THE LITTLE BOOK OF

Bordeaux Wines

GW00707734

Bruno Boidron

Flammarion

The Story of
Bordeaux Wines 6

Alphabetical Guide 18

Appendices

Alphabetical Guide

The alphabetical entries have been classified according to the following categories. Each category is indicated with a small colored square.

■ Famous Appellations

Barsac
Blaye, Côtes de Blaye, Premières Côtes de Blaye
Bordeaux & Bordeaux Supérieur
Bordeaux Clairet
Bordeaux Côtes de Francs
Bordeaux Rosé
Cadillac
Cérons
Côtes de Bordeaux Saint-Macaire
Côtes de Bourg, Bourg, Bourgeais
Côtes de Castillon

Crémant de Bordeaux
Entre-deux-Mers & Entre-deux-Mers Haut-Benauge
Fronsac & Canon-Fronsac
Graves & Graves Supérieures
Graves de Vayres
Haut-Médoc
Lalande-de-Pomerol
Listrac-Médoc
Loupiac
Lussac-Saint-Émilion
Margaux
Médoc
Montagne-Saint-Émilion
Moulis

Pauillac
Pessac-Léognan
Pomerol
Premières Côtes de Bordeaux
Puisseguin-Saint-Émilion
Saint-Émilion & Saint-Émilion Grand Cru
Saint-Estèphe
Saint-Georges-Saint-Émilion
Saint-Julien
Sainte-Croix-du-Mont
Sainte-Foy-Bordeaux
Sauternes

■ The Keys to the Vineyard

Academy
Aging
Appellation area
Blends
Bordeaux oak casks
Botrytis cinerea
Brokers
CIVB – Conseil Interprofessionnel du Vin de Bordeaux

Crus and brands
Fraternities
Girondins
Investors
Primeur
Rivers
Serving wine
Tannin
Tasting
Terroir

Tonneau
Tourism
Union des Grands Crus
Wine trade

■ Famous *Crus* (growths)

Bélair (Ch.)
Belgrave (Ch.)
Beychevelle (Ch.)
Bonnet (Ch.)
Cheval Blanc (Ch.)
Closiot (Ch.)
Côte Montpezat (Ch.)
Ducru Beaucaillou (Ch.)
Escurac (Ch. d')
Grand-Mouëys (Ch.)

Guiraud (Ch.)
Haut-Brion (Ch.)
Haut-Marbuzet (Ch.)
Latour (Ch.)
Latour Martillac (Ch.)
Maison Blanche (Ch.)
Margaux (Ch.)
Mondésir Gazin (Ch.)
Montrose (Ch.)
Moulin Haut-Laroque (Ch.)

Mouton Rothschild (Ch.)
Nodoz (Ch.)
Pétrus (Ch.)
Poujeaux (Ch.)
Puygueraud (Ch.)
Rame (Ch. la)
Seuil (Ch. du)
Tour Haut-Caussan (Ch.)
Vieux Château Gaubert
Yquem (Ch. d')

The information given in each entry, together with cross-references indicated by asterisks, enables the reader to explore the world of Bordeaux wines.

THE STORY OF BORDEAUX WINES

The origins of Bordeaux wines are unquestionably Roman. Archeological digs conducted in recent years have shown that vineyards existed in Bordeaux before 40 B.C. There is no doubt today that Bordeaux wine has entered its third millennium. Wine lovers, as they read this book, will soon realize that the history of Bordeaux wines is inseparable from those of its appellations and *crus* (growths). There is not one history, but many individual stories. The cultivation of vines in Bordeaux has spawned much more than the wine itself, and any brief summary is necessarily inadequate.

Stele of a male innkeeper: late second or early third century.

L'AMPHITHEATRE DE BOVRDEAVS,

DIVERSITY AND ADVERSITY: THE CLASSIFICATIONS

During its history Bordeaux has produced about fifty appellations and the region still boasts some seven thousand *crus*. Both a handicap and a blessing, this great diversity needs some selection and explanation before it can be understood by wine enthusiasts and buyers.

As a result of factors such as the quality of the soil and subsoil, grape varieties, techniques used, and human skill, some *crus* gain such fame that they are considered to be the best of their appellation or of their area at a given time.

Bordeaux Amphitheater, nineteenth century (Palais Gallien), quarto wood engraving in *Commentaire d'Ausone* by Vinet, 1575–1580.

Before this happens, though, and regardless of the quality of the wine, a number of criteria are applied to establish a classification and place the wine in a context. Even so, any classification is relative and can be disputed. A *cru* which has been neglected by an impoverished owner could be taken over by someone who is active, dynamic, wealthy and, most importantly, competent, and might begin to produce better wine. But the opposite could happen just as easily.

Therefore, classifications must be considered only in terms of the factors used to establish them. Similarly, it is important not to confuse tastings*, which are held at various intervals, with these criteria. Even if they are subject to time, the classifications take into account elements that owe nothing to the palates of wine experts and gurus.

Based on the notion of *crus*, which was established in the seventeenth century—the first step towards creating an official ranking—the classification system for Gironde wines is unlike any other. The Bordeaux wine market is governed by a simple system involving three roles: the broker*, the merchant, and the owner. By the eighteenth century this system already allowed brokers, who held a privileged role, to establish ratings for different wines. This relied not only on the brokers' tasting skills but also, particularly, on their knowledge of the vineyards. The concepts of "*Grand Cru*" and "*Second Cru*," which took shape from the beginning of the eighteenth century in the main vineyards (Haut-Brion*, Margaux*, Latour*, Lafite, etc.), are a result of their qualitative assessments of the various *terroirs* (soil and growing conditions).

The first books to draw on this professional knowledge were published in the early nineteenth century by the authors A. Jullien (1816), W. Franck (1824), and C. Cocks (1846), who wrote the first edition of the famous Féret wine guide.

These documents are revealing in more ways than one. They clearly show that during this period the wines of the Médoc* and Sauternes* dominated the market. These were worth twice as much as those from Graves* and three times as much as wines from Saint-Émilion*. Interestingly, this classification system—which is still officially used—remains accurate today.

In 1855 the Bordeaux Chamber of Commerce, wishing to present the wines of the Gironde at the Universal Exhibition in Paris, sought a way for this to be done as fairly as possible. To avoid having the wines judged by uneducated palates, the Chamber did not enter them in contests and presented them according to a precise classification system. The Chamber asked the brokers'

union to provide a "complete list of classified red Bordeaux wines, as well as of the great white wines." On April 18, 1855 the brokers' union presented its classification, which consisted of two lists entitled "Classified red wines of the Gironde" and "Classified white wines of the Gironde." Far from being the result of a single tasting or a periodic evaluation of the market, these lists were, on the contrary, a synthesis of the brokers' considerable practical and statistical knowledge—their profession was by then more than 150 years old. In their ranking were included only the wines of the Médoc*, the sweet white wines of Sauternes* and Barsac*, and Château Haut-Brion* in Pessac (Graves*).

Portrait of Germain Rambaud (1732–1822), Barton and Guestier's cellarmaster from 1755 to 1815.

Old house
on the
Château
de Jayle
property,
eighteenth
century.

Bottom:
Uprooting
infected
vines in the
Médoc, early
twentieth
century.

The second classification to be established was that of Graves*
wines in 1953. At the request of the Union for the Defense of
the Graves AOC (*Appellation d'Origine Contrôlée,* a warranty of
the wine's origin), the Institut National des Appellations d'Origine (INAO) created a classification for this region's growths
which was approved by the French minister of agriculture
in 1953.

This cannot be compared to the 1855 classification, as it was
carried out under different conditions and was based on different
factors. The list makes a distinction between the two types of
production in this region: red and white wines are classified sepa-
rately. Today all the classified Graves belong to an AOC created
in 1993, Pessac-Léognan*.

The last classification is that of Saint-Emilion*. Not until 1958, after multiple requests, did the winemakers of Saint-Emilion succeed in having an official classification published, which allowed the best *crus* of this region to benefit from the title "*Cru Classé.*" Established by decree, the classification of Saint-Émilion *crus* is unlike those that preceded it. The decree stipulates that the classification be revised every decade—this was done in 1969, in 1986, and again in 1996.

Two other classifications complete the picture. Realizing that the 1855 list could not be revised, certain winemakers in the

Château Lacouspaude, *Grand Cru Classé.*

Médoc*, such as Philippe de Rothschild, asked the Chamber of Commerce to create a contest which would reward their efforts with their *terroir**, allowing new titles to be awarded. The contest, held in 1973, was open only to *crus* classified in 1855 and applied only to the category "*Premiers Crus.*" An order of the Ministry of Agriculture announced the 1973 list of "*Premiers Crus Classés*"—this was identical to the 1855 classification except for the addition of Château Mouton-Rothschild*.

Still in Médoc, as early as 1932, a category called "*Crus Bourgeois*" was created by five wine brokers* who were also

merchants. A 1972 law calls for a contest to create and update a ranking system for Bordeaux wines produced by *crus* in the geographical area defined by the AOC Médoc*. It specifies that the titles to be awarded will be: "*Crus Bourgeois Exceptionnels,*" "*Crus Grands Bourgeois,*" and "*Crus Bourgeois.*"

As far as we know the contest for *Crus Bourgeois* has not yet been held, but could take place before the end of the year 2001. This would allow the consumer to understand better the use of the term *Cru Bourgeois*, which would be used for *crus* and not for brands*, and would offer a guarantee of quality.

Thomas Barton's cellar.

BORDEAUX: A CENTER FOR SCIENTIFIC RESEARCH

The French national institute for agronomic research (INRA) has greatly contributed to the efforts of wine research teams and local oenologists belonging to various organizations who want to improve the efficiency of their work.

First, the *Institut de la Vigne de Bordeaux* (Institute of the Bordeaux Vine) was created, bringing together the research units of the Bordeaux-Aquitaine INRA center and the University of Bordeaux Laboratory of Sciences. More recently, researchers from the Faculty of Oenology at the University of Bordeaux and those of the

Bordeaux, bridge over the Garonne, Quai de Bourgogne and Quai de la Bourse; Terpereau negative from *Géographie pittoresque et monumentale de la France*, 1902.

Institut de la Vigne came together to form the "pole of scientific research on the vine and wine," an association of sixty specialists in the production of top quality wines representing every profession concerned.

A University of Wine is being planned for the near future in Bordeaux, to be directed by the region's scientists and researchers. It will symbolize the vigor and capacity for innovation demonstrated by the entire Bordeaux wine industry.

THE BORDEAUX WINE MARKET

The world's biggest producer of quality wines, Bordeaux also has the world's largest wine trade. Figures show that the Bordeaux market is close to reaching a balance of employment and resources. With the help of well-established merchants, Bordeaux ships its wines each year to the four corners of the world, in a volume about equal to its production, but it is possible that a year of severe frost such as 1991 could lead to a wine shortage.

Bordeaux is increasing its exports, which represent about 35 percent of the volume put on the market. Four countries that have traditionally imported Bordeaux—Belgium, Germany, the United Kingdom, and the Netherlands—buy about sixty percent of this volume. The United States, Denmark, Canada,

Switzerland, and Japan also belong to the core group of importers. Most Bordeaux wine is sold within France, however, and eighty percent of this is distributed by major superstores. Small, independent dealers still survive in many towns, though, and have their own clientele who would not shop anywhere else.

In the face of rapidly growing competition from foreign producers, many people today wonder what will become of Bordeaux wines. Will their reputation ensure their survival? The answer lies in the quality of the wines, which thanks to regional investment in technology and research, can only improve.

White wine bottles chilling.

Academy

Founded on April 17, 1948 by a group of key personalities among the merchants* and growers, the *Académie du Vin de Bordeaux* (Bordeaux Wine Academy) is uniquely qualified to preserve and promote the spirit, history, and culture of Bordeaux wine in France and abroad.

Aging

The question of aging remains an enigma for many wine-lovers. In the past, a large number of French households were equipped with cellars, making it easy to age wines. Because of this, wine-growers were in the habit of making hard, tannic, deeply colored wines that were practically undrinkable in their youth.

Statues of the Muses, Grand Théâtre, Bordeaux.

The cultivation of the vine in Bordeaux has not only produced wines which are universally recognized, but has also profoundly shaped the lifestyle of the Gironde. The result is a particular form of humanism, a spirit, an ethic, and a striving for perfection that can be felt the world over.

Like the prestigious *Académie Française* in Paris, the Bordeaux Academy—the most prestigious representative of Bordeaux wines—has forty members. Among these are the owners of the most celebrated *crus* in Bordeaux, but there are also two members of the *Académie Française*, writers, artists, scholars, and university professors.

Today, the rarity of proper cellars and the financial cost of accumulating wines to drink later have made younger wines popular with consumers, even if many wine-lovers appreciate old vintages.

This trend has led growers to produce suppler wines that are drinkable after a few years but that also improve if they are kept longer. They were able to do this by careful blending and adjustment of the vinification techniques. It is difficult, then, to know when is the best time to drink any given wine. As this depends on the taste of each person, the only solution is to buy enough of each wine to be able to taste it at regular intervals in order to decide when it is at its peak.

APPELLATION AREA

This is the exclusive and strictly defined area in which vines must grow in order for the wines they produce to earn the AOC title.

■ BARSAC (A.O.C.)

The privilege of royal provostship, awarded to Barsac in the thirteenth century, greatly contributed to the development of its vineyards, and thus to its renown. Located at the mouth of the Ciron river, Barsac is blessed with an exceptional microclimate which provides a natural breeding ground for "noble rot:" the much-prized fungal growth *botrytis cinerea**. Barsac's famous landscape is easily recognizable thanks to the dry stone walls which surround the vineyards. Two types of soil here are ideal for viticulture: alluvial deposits which form gravelly soils (a type of gravel known as Garonne Günz), and a plateau of clay-limestone overlaying limestone, the site of the oldest *crus*.

Ten of this town's *crus* were classified in 1855, and two were named *Premiers Crus* (First Growths): Cimens and Coutet. Among the *crus* of special interest to wine enthusiasts in this AOC, classified or not, are those of Châteaux Broustet, Doisy, Védrines, Piada, Liot, and Closiot*.

Barsac AOC wines are remarkable for their beautiful golden color ranging from pale gold to yellow gold. The nose is full and deep. Varied and fruity aromas develop: acacia honey, vanilla, white peach flesh, sweet almond—and especially botrytized grapes, which become increasingly complex and harmonious over time, producing aromas such as dried apricot and candied orange. The knowledgeable taster will detect a vigorous strength which enlivens the syrupy sweetness of Barsac wines to create a complex blend of liqueur and alcohol, and an unequaled balance.

Due to an anomaly in the Sauternes region's appellation system, growers may choose to label their wines with the Barsac or the Sauternes* AOC.

A dry stone wall in the Sauternes region.

Château Bélair,
nineteenth-
century
engraving.

▪ Bélair (Ch.)

Château Bélair has always been classified among the best of Saint-Emilion's First Growths, and its origins are ancient. During the period of Bordeaux's allegiance to the British crown, the property belonged to Robert de Knolles, the great seneschal and governor of Guyenne, who owned a considerable amount of land in the region. This worthy captain, who fought in the Battle of the Thirty in 1351, also took part in the battles of Avray and Navarette; this is where he received his insignia of honor when he was awarded Bertrand Du Guesclin's sword. When Charles VII won back Guyenne, the descendants of Robert de Knolles remained on his land. They made their name French, changing it to Canolle, and kept the property until the French Revolution. The land was then taken over by another family, but was later restored to its original owners. After the sister of Marquis Robert de Canolle married Baron Seissan de Marignan, the baron received a share of Bélair.

The Château Bélair *cru* owes its undeniable superiority to the unusual nature of the terrain as well as its fortunate orientation to the south and the east: celebrated wines have been produced here for centuries. Among their most prestigious awards have been the Gold Medal at the 1889 Universal Exhibition, and the *Diplôme de Grand Prix* at the Paris Exhibition in 1900. Château Bélair, *Premier Grand Cru Classé B*, adjoins Ausone and has been owned since 1916 by the Dubois-Challon family. The winemaking facilities are unusual for their massive proportions; the wine is made using the force of gravity. This was the first gravitational winery in Bordeaux.

▪ Belgrave (Ch.)

Château Belgrave is one of the oldest Haut-Médoc* *crus*. The property is dominated by a handsome hunting lodge built in the eighteenth century; a long white path lined with umbrella pines leads to its peaceful grounds. The 56-hectare vineyard surrounds the château and the winery.

Classified a Fifth Growth in 1855 for the quality of the soil, with its gravelly ridges, Belgrave suffered as a result of the difficult period that followed World War II.

Acquired by a group of agricultural investors in 1979, the land was placed under the management of the CVBG group (Dourthe-Kressmann), which immediately began a vast rehabilitation program.

The first step was to create winemaking facilities at Château Belgrave which befitted a *cru** of this quality. These were completed in 1990 with the installation of an electronic thermo-regulation system for the *cuvier*, which holds the vats. By 1980, a storehouse with the capacity to hold 1,500 Bordeaux oak casks* had been built alongside the *cuvier*. At the same time, around ten hectares of vineyard were being renewed.

The second stage, starting in 1986, was marked by the involvement of Professor Alain Reynier in the running of the vineyard and of Michel Rolland in the winemaking, selection, and maturation.

These investments soon bore fruit. The 1995 Gault Millau guide rated Château Belgrave above its official classification.

The château itself underwent a remarkable restoration in 1992 and 1993. Restored, modernized, and once again recognized, Château Belgrave re-established its rightful place among the elite of Médoc* wines.

This château is a member of the *Union des Grands Crus**.

Château Belgrave, whose wine was classified in 1855.

■ Beychevelle (Ch.)

Always the territory of powerful men, Beychevelle boasts a long and rich history. During the Middle Ages, when it was owned by the counts of Foix-Candale, the wine was shipped from the port at the bottom of the garden. Bishop François de Foix-Candale had a first château built in 1565. He was followed by Jean-Louis de Nogaret de la Valette, first Duc d'Épernon and Admiral of France, his son Bernard who added the central portion of the château in 1644, then Henri de Foix-Candale. In the eighteenth century, the property belonged successively to Jean-Baptiste d'Abadie, President of the Bordeaux parliament; to the Brassier family who partially rebuilt the château, giving the building its present form; and to the ship-owner Jacques Conte. The nineteenth century was dedicated to the re-establishment of quality and renown thanks to Pierre-François Guestier, a Bordeaux merchant and mayor of Saint-Julien, and to Armand Heine (cousin of the German poet Heinrich Heine) and his wife, Marie-Amélie Kohn, who restored this vineyard to greatness. Three generations of the Achille-Fould family succeeded each other at Beychevelle over the next century until it was acquired in 1986 by GMF, the French civil servants' pension fund. In 1989 GMF established a partnership with the Japanese group Suntory to create the company, Grands Millésimes de France, which is the current owner.

Legend has it that ships passing the château lowered their sails to pay homage to the all-powerful Duc d'Épernon—

hence the name Beychevelle, from the phrase *baisse-voile* (lower sail), and the origin of the château's arms.

Château Beychevelle, classified a Fourth Growth in 1855, produces 500 *tonneaux** of wine with the Saint-Julien AOC. Very delicate, with complex aromas, its wines have won great respect in France and abroad.

◼ Blaye, Côtes de Blaye, Premières Côtes de Blaye (A.O.C.)

The origins of the city of Blaye go back to earliest antiquity. Around 25 B.C., the Romans established a fort here to act as a shield for Bordeaux. Later, Blaye became part of the defense system for Bordeaux designed by Sébastien Le Prestre de Vauban, the marshal in charge of fortifications during the seventeenth century. Today this perfectly preserved citadel is a popular tourist* attraction. The region is lush and pleasant. In the south, steep vine-covered slopes overlook the Gironde, while in the north the river* is bordered by marshes. On the eastern extremity, the forest seems to be gradually gaining ground.

Château Beychevelle, classified in 1855.

25

Most of the vineyards in this region have belonged to the same family for three or four generations, sometimes more. The size of the vineyards is quite variable. Good value for money, Blaye wines are following the lead of neighboring Bourg in finding a respected name for themselves among wine-growing regions.

Because of stricter production conditions, wines with the Premières Côtes de Blaye AOC—including Château Peyrère, Château Mondésir Gazin*, and Château l'Escadre—are generally better quality than those with the labels Blaye, Blayais, or Côtes de Blaye AOC.

The red wines have an attractive color and pronounced fruitiness, and are supple with a pleasant bouquet. As they age, the color changes to brick and, depending on the grape varieties, aromas of musk or spices develop. Supple and fresh, the white wines are distinctive for the quality and diversity of their aromas.

Blends

Without being specific to Bordeaux, this practice is typical of the region: wines of various grape varieties and from different vats, but of the same AOC, are blended to produce a single wine of as consistent a quality as possible, which will be marketed under the name of the wine estate.

This apparently simple blending is in reality a crucial and particularly delicate operation, which must be carried out with a great deal of care and perceptiveness. Upon it will depend the greater or lesser quality of the vintage. During this procedure, the taster's assessment, sensory memory, and ability

The *Kaskelot* sailing on the Garonne, between Blaye and Bourg.

27

to predict how the wine will develop as it ages play a role that no machine could begin to replace.

■ Bonnet (Ch.)

Château Bonnet is located north of Entre-Deux-Mers* on the clay-limestone outcrops of the Grézillac commune, which overlooks the Dordogne valley about ten kilometers south of Saint-Emilion. In the seventeenth century, Château Bonnet belonged to Pierre de Reynier, Lord of Barre and Bonnet, and former captain of the Royal Regiment of Normandy. On September 17, 1744, Jean de Chillaud des Fieux, adviser to the King and the Court's representative for petitions to the Palace, acquired the property.

At this time the land already had an extensive vineyard, judging from the size of the stone wine presses whose remains can be seen today. His son, Jacques Justin, inherited Bonnet in 1786. He demolished the old manor and built the current château, which was completed in 1788.

Pursued during the French Revolution, Jacques de Chillaud hid in a well in one of the château's outbuildings. This well has now been restored. Called plain Jacques Chillaud (without the noble "de") after he gave up his title, he sold Bonnet and its 100 hectares of land in 1810 to Eugène Lavignac, who had made his fortune in the colonies. On November 11, 1880, Eugène Lavignac's son sold Bonnet to Etienne Brunetière, who in turn sold it to Léonce Récapet on December 30, 1897. He was one of the most important wine growers of his era and one of the trail-blazers in the replanting of the Bordeaux vineyards after they were devastated by

phylloxera. He established 120 hectares of vineyards around Bonnet.

One of his grandsons, André Lurton, took over the ownership of the château in 1956 when only thirty hectares of vines remained and worked hard to re-establish and develop the vineyards planted by his grandfather.

Today, fifty percent of the wine produced by these vineyards is a much-appreciated dry white Entre-Deux-Mers*. These wines are made very carefully to preserve all the freshness of the fruit. Also on the land are extensive vineyards which produce a red Bordeaux* considered to be far above average for its AOC. A large part of the harvest is matured in cask. This explains the use of two labels for the red Château Bonnet: one matured in cask, called "traditional," and the other bottled a little younger

and called "classic." Bonnet now consists of a vast wine-growing property which in certain years can produce, with its offshoots, more than 1,300 *tonneaux** of wine.

Traditional oak casks.

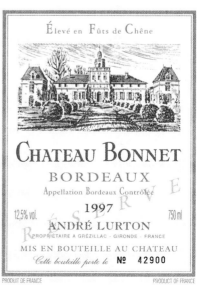

■ BORDEAUX & BORDEAUX SUPÉRIEUR, BORDEAUX ROSÉ & BORDEAUX CLAIRET (A.O.C.)

The Bordeaux and Bordeaux Supérieur AOCs are the largest of the French AOCs in terms of both surface area and volume: more than 50,000 hectares (44 percent of the region's vineyards) produce more than three million hectoliters annually.

Their surface area is equal to the total surface area of all the other appellations in the region.

The only way to describe these wines is to speak of the diversity of the *terroirs** (soil and conditions) covered by the title. The vast range of *terroirs** is united by the vision and passion of the men who grow the grapes and make the wine.

To describe a Bordeaux AOC wine fully, you would need to speak of each of the two thousand vineyards covered by the label. Red Bordeaux wines are easy to drink: they can be supple, fruity, or rich, depending on the vintage.

Bordeaux AOC wines can be enjoyed young, while Bordeaux Supérieur AOC wines develop charm and fullness as they age.

These wines are always welcome, their lack of pretension expressing the generosity and warmth of the Gironde region.

Bordeaux rosé and Bordeaux clairet are distinguishable by the rosé's pale pink color, and the clairet's stronger pink. After macerating briefly with the grape skins, these wines are made in the same way as white Bordeaux. Bordeaux clairet wines are, in fact, worthy descendants of "French clarets,"

the first type of wine to be made in the region.

Dry white Bordeaux are generally pale in color but fruity and gently perfumed. Their natural freshness gives them a strength which goes perfectly with seafood.

Bordeaux Supérieur wines are subject to stricter conditions of production and vinification: the permitted yield is ten percent smaller than for AOC Bordeaux, and they must have matured for at least a year before being put on the market; some even spend time in Bordeaux oak casks*. All have the characteristics of a quality wine, with potential for aging, and prices that will not break the bank of wine-lovers. White Bordeaux Supérieur wines are made with blends* identical to those of white Bordeaux. However, over-ripe grapes are used, which make them richer in alcohol and in sugar. They are generally sweeter and smoother.

Worth a mention among the best-known *crus* are Châteaux Seguin, Parenchère, Tour de Mirambeau, Thieuly, and Bonnet*.

■ Bordeaux Côtes de Francs (A.O.C.)

The village of Francs, for which this AOC is named, is located near the border of the Dordogne region.

Its origins go back to the sixth century. In 507, after the Battle of Vouillé, Clovis I, King of the Francs, fought Alaric II, King of the Visigoths, and conquered the region of Aquitaine. A detachment of the Frankish army set up camp on the site of the village, which was named "Ad Francos" and later Francs.

As in neighboring regions, vines have been planted here since ancient times. Far from major highways, the region is calm and pleasant. Its hills, often capped with ruins of windmills and

Their average surface area is usually more than ten hectares. These are often planted with more than fifty percent Merlot, followed by Cabernet Franc, Cabernet Sauvignon, and occasionally Malbec. Among the best of the châteaux are Puygueraud*, Prévot, Puy, and Marsau.

The red wines—opulent, rich, and deeply colored—are remarkable for the harmony and femininity of their tannins*. They are an excellent choice for the cellar. However, depending on the vintage, they can be particularly pleasant when drunk young, thanks to their elegant note of red berries. The white wines, which can be dry or sweet, also show character.

Judging Botrytis Cinerea by its smell during the harvest.

dovecots, are covered in vines; in the lower part of the valley are meadows and farmland.

Though this region can produce both red and white wines, most of the vineyards produce red wines.

■ Bordeaux oak casks

The best red Bordeaux are matured in *barriques*, oak casks which hold 225 liters. These barrels also come in smaller sizes, the half-cask and quarter cask.

BOTRYTIS CINEREA

Botrytis cinerea is a fungus found throughout the world which can attack many different plants. Alternate periods of rain and sun encourage its development.

Depending on the situation, the season, and its development, *Botrytis* can give rise to gray or vulgar rot, the bane of the winemaker's existence, but also to the noble rot which is so desirable in the making of sweet wines.

Due to the fact that it attacks ripe and even over-ripe grapes which are healthy and intact, *Botrytis* concentrates the sugar content of the berry, which shrinks in size while the skin turns brown. The grape is still swollen and full, which is the "full rot" stage.

With the return of hotter and drier weather, the growth of the fungus around the berry slows down and no longer shows signs of spreading.

The berry then turns a purple-brown color, wrinkles, folds, and shrinks—in short, over-ripens—as a result of the *Botrytis* which, as it nourishes itself on part of the grape's sap, concentrates and increases the levels of sugar, glycerine, and other elements, thus reducing the acidity.

The juice can have a sugar content as high as 300 to 350 grams per liter— sometimes more.

In turn, the volume of the yield can shrink by fifty percent or more. A grape that has been attacked by *Botrytis* is dead: it is no longer nourished by the vine.

Brokers

Brokers' perfect knowledge of the region allow them to act as go-betweens for the grower and merchant. They advise buyers and sellers and make sure that there are no disputes between them; they never do a deal for themselves.

Cadillac (A.O.C.)

Cadillac is a very ancient town; part of it is still enclosed by the ruins of a wall erected in 1280 by Jean de Grailly, Mayor of Buch. The town contains the château of the Ducs d'Épernon, built between 1600 and 1650.

Created in 1973, the Cadillac AOC has undergone dramatic changes. It is classified for its sweet white wines, which must come from over-ripe grapes affected by noble rot that have been picked in a series of selective harvests. The soil has the same composition as that of the Premières Côtes de Bordeaux*, to which it belongs.

AOC Cadillac wines have similar qualities to the wines of Sainte-Croix-du-Mont*. Like the latter, they are elegant, perfumed, and fruity.

Typical of their appellation, the Châteaux La Clyde, La Bertrande, Melin, and Clos Sainte Anne produce delightful wines.

Cérons (A.O.C.)

A resting point for soldiers and traders, Sirione (Cérons) is the only place to have been cited on both Antonin's Itinerary, a map of the road

Château de Cadillac.

system under Emperor Caracalla (211–217), and on the "Tabula Peutingeriana," a thirteenth-century copy of a Roman map of the empire's third-century military roads.

This favored site in the Graves region is shaped by the vast plateau which contains the communes of Cérons, Pondensac, and Illats. In 1935, when AOCs were established, the region was awarded two: Graves*, and Cérons for its sweet white wines.

Since 1988, encouraged by a slight increase in demand for sweet wines and aware of the wine's illustrious past, some growers have produced a few hectoliters of AOC Cérons each year; among these are Château Cérons and Château Grand Enclos de Cérons.

The geographic location of this region combined with the superb quality of its wines have led Bordeaux's merchants—who are the best judges in these matters—to say that the wines of Cérons are the real link between the best wines of Graves* and the sweet white wines of Barsac* and Sauternes*.

■ Cheval Blanc (Ch.)

A Saint-Emilion* *Premier Grand Cru Classé A*, Château Cheval Blanc is located on the border of Saint-Émilion and Pomerol. This property is characterized by a curious mix of soils and subsoils which seems to change at every step. Here, it is dense earth over clay; there, sandy soil over clay streaked with iron, or gravelly soil.

Because of this diversity, combined with a judicious choice of grape varieties and careful attention to viticulture and winemaking, Cheval Blanc wines are extremely mellow, full-bodied, and delicate, with a delicious bouquet. Above all, they have a personality which makes them always recognizable, and increasingly in demand.

The property covers an area of 36 hectares, unchanged since 1850. The owners have improved it in every conceivable way—better drainage, plant selection, storerooms—while maintaining the grape varieties and as many old vines as possible, which explains the ever-greater quality of the wines.

Château Cheval Blanc.

▢ CIVB
Conseil Interprofessionnel du Vin de Bordeaux
(Interprofessional Council of Bordeaux Wine)

The idea of a joint-trade organization for Bordeaux was first proposed by F. Ginestet, an owner and merchant, after World War I. It initially took shape as an association: the *Union de la Proprieté et du Commerce* (Union of Property and Trade). Only after World War II, on the initiative of Girondin* members of parliament (including the Vice-president of the National Assembly, E. Liquard), did the state create, by a law dated August 18, 1948, the *Conseil Interprofessionnel du Vin de Bordeaux.*

Its three defined objectives are:

1. To carry out studies and develop proposed regulations concerning the orientation, regularization, and organization of the Bordeaux wine market

2. To build, in France and abroad, the reputation and the demand for AOC Bordeaux wines

3. To ensure the application and effective enforcement of the AOC requirements, in order to guarantee consumers that the quality of a Bordeaux wine will correspond to its appellation.

CIVB building in Bordeaux.

■ Closiot (Ch.)

This property has a rich and eventful past. Its name was mentioned for the first time in 1766 in a notarized deed concerning the sale of lands in Barsac* between the heirs of the Marquis de Montferrand and Laurent de Sauvage d'Yquem. This official document stipulated "the land of Clouziot, with vines." Joséphine, the daughter and sole heir of Laurent de Sauvage, married Count Louis Amédée de Lur-Saluces in 1785. Sadly, he died three years after the wedding and his wife had considerable difficulty holding on to the property during the Revolution.

In 1850, Château Closiot was cited in the first edition of the Féret guide to Bordeaux wines. It was included in each successive edition under the category Second Growths. Renamed "Clos Bonneau" by its owner, it appeared in the 1881 Féret with the name "Clos Bonneau-Clouiscot."

After a period as Clos Bonneau Closiot from 1893, the property was definitively named Château Closiot in 1898.

Twenty-five years later it was acquired by Alban Duprat, the maternal grandfather of the current owner, Françoise Sirot-Soizeau. This former stopping place on the pilgrimage way to Saint James of Compostela has now been run by the same family for three generations. Seeking to develop the property, Françoise's father Hector bought Château Camperos, also located in Barsac, in 1961.

Françoise took over the reins of the family business in 1988. Not afraid to adapt to modern realities, she has invested a great deal in the vineyard: planting new vines, a return to working the land, renovated storehouses, a modernized *cuvier*, oak barrels* which are renewed by a third each year, a temperature-controlled bottle cellar, and renovated reception buildings.

Respectful of traditions but also of recent technological advances, Françoise and her husband, Bernard Sirot, can count on the expertise of a cellarmaster and a wine-grower who, during the harvest, work with some fifteen grape-pickers. Group meals and a family atmosphere win the loyalty of these workers, who are responsible for the intrinsic quality of the wines.

Château Closiot.

■ Côte Montpezat (Ch.)

Dating from the very beginning of the seventeenth century, as the date carved above the fireplace prove, this property can rightly be proud of its rich and very long history.

In the middle of the domain is an old well, which still resounds with voices and peals of laughter. If you listen carefully, it tells of the joys and sorrows of pilgrims on their way to Saint James of Compostela who, from the tenth to the fifteenth centuries, stopped here to quench their thirst.

These days the waters are just as pure, but their level is a little lower. This is because the property's owner, like Jesus at the wedding at Cana, contemplated the vineyard's potential and used his powers to change water into wine. Like the pilgrims of the Middle Ages, the vine stocks soak up strength, vigor, and sap from this generous *terroir**.

But, if nature allows us to work miracles, it does require our assistance! That's why, wishing to make this estate one of the best, if not the best, of the Côtes-de-Castillon*, its owner has endowed it with modern and functional equipment worthy of the most prestigious estates. The resulting wine is not only seductive and fruity, but a fine wine which benefits from aging* (in oak casks* and bottles), and has a strong personality.

■ Côtes de Bordeaux Saint-Macaire (A.O.C.)

A part of Bordeaux in medieval times, Saint-Macaire owes its name to a bishop who preached here during the sixth century. It is a very interesting and curious town which has much to offer the visitor.

The Côtes de Bordeaux-Saint Macaire region begins at the eastern tip of the Premières Côtes de Bordeaux.

Only the white wines are entitled to the AOC Côtes de Bordeaux Saint-Macaire. Their reputation goes back a long way, thanks to the nature of the soil and the care that goes into their making. They are generally refined and fairly rich, but supple—often sweet and sometimes syrupy, depending on the *cru**. Château Fayard and Château Malromé are worth seeking out for their quality.

Growers devote a large part of their vineyards to red wine; these vines generally produce wines with the AOC Bordeaux or Bordeaux Supérieur appellation.

Premières Côtes de Bordeaux vineyard.

Bourg vineyard.

■ Côtes de Bourg, Bourg, Bourgeais (A.O.C.)

Bourg-sur-Gironde, for which this AOC is named, is located on the right bank of the Dordogne. In 1379, during English rule, Bordeaux formed a close alliance with eight neighboring towns which were walled or fortified. This is how Bourg-sur-Gironde became a part of Bordeaux. During the Fronde, a seventeenth-century uprising against Cardinal Mazarin, the ruling monarch Queen Anne of Austria stayed here for a time with Louis XIV (then aged twelve), Cardinal Mazarin and their court. During this time, Anne of Austria and her ladies embroidered cloths for the altar; these are now on display at the town hall.

Because of its proximity to the river, Bourg has always been a center for trade. According to certain authors, vines might have been planted in the region from the time of the Roman conquest, around the first century B.C.

Under English rule, despite the tensions between the two kingdoms, the vineyards multiplied, and full shiploads of wine left Bourg for England. From the fifteenth to the eighteenth century, this wine-growing region continued to expand.

The Bourgeais region consists of a series of hills, some of them steep, often ending in sharp cliffs on the banks of rivers*.

Clay-limestone or clay gravel soils cover a limestone subsoil which is often very hard.

Red Côtes de Bourg AOC wines are richly colored: dark red, intense, and vivid. Strong but still supple, they have a fresh quality and a distinctive bouquet due to the soils in which the vines are grown. Because of their structure, these wines can be appreciated young for their fruit. White Côtes de Bourg are dry, fresh, and fruity. The Châteaux Nodoz*, Croute Coupon, de Barbe, and Caruel also deserve a special mention.

Referring to the same wine, the names Bourg and Bourgeais are no longer used because wine-growers prefer the Côtes de Bourg appellation.

■ Côtes de Castillon (A.O.C.)

The town of Castillon-la-Bataille, for which this AOC is named, refers to the famous Battle of Castillon which, in 1453, put an end to the Hundred Years' War. John de Talbot, who led the English army, was killed there.

The sites of certain villas and Gallo-Roman mosaics show that vines were planted here in Roman times.

This appellation zone is outlined by hills, which start where Saint-Émilion ends, and grow smaller towards the east. Some of the hills are more than 100 meters high, giving wide views of this vine-covered region, interspersed with small valleys where various other crops grow. The climate here is agreeable, as the winds are not too strong and the coastal influence is slight. Together, these conditions make for a *terroir** ideally suited to wine-growing.

Only the red wines can use the Côtes de Castillon AOC; among these, Château Cap de Faugères and Château Côte Montpezat are excellent ambassadors.

Vines in winter.

■ CRÉMANT DE BORDEAUX (A.O.C.)

Conscious that sparkling AOC Bordeaux wines produced according to traditional methods are original and unique, winemakers and professionals in Bordeaux decided to apply rigorous rules to the making of these wines.

Thus was born the Crémant de Bordeaux AOC in 1990. These sparkling wines are fine and perfumed, very pleasant as an apéritif, to round off a meal, or even with food. Made with white Bordeaux that meets the AOC requirements, and sometimes with the must of red grapes used to make white wines, crémants have less of a reputation than other sparkling AOC wines that are made in a similar way—this is due to the small quantity of Crémant de Bordeaux produced. The term *méthode champenoise* was once used, but because this type of winemaking is specific to Champagne, the expression is now reserved for wines with the Champagne AOC. Beyond the label itself, real efforts that have gone into the making of Crémant de Bordeaux have helped win over consumers who appreciate lively, fresh, fruity wines and attractive presentation.

CRUS AND BRANDS

It is important to make a distinction between two ideas fundamental to the concept of *cru* in Bordeaux. The first, *cru*, refers to the whole production entity: the vineyards, cellars, and a residence. Inseparable from this production entity is the wine brand, which should be the only name to include terms such as "château," "domaine," or "clos."

But since the market requires that brands be purely commercial, many brands (lower-quality wines, distributors' brands, etc.) use terms such as "château," thus continuing to create confusion in the customer's mind.

Ducru Beaucaillou (Ch.)

Classified as a Second Growth in 1855, Château Beaucaillou is usually called Ducru-Beaucaillou, after its former owner, Monsieur Ducru.

Its history, like that of all the great growths of the Médoc, goes back to the end of the seventeenth and beginning of the eighteenth century. During the Revolution, Monsieur Bergeron was the owner. Nathaniel Johnston, one of a well-known family of Bordeaux wine merchants, bought the property from the Ducru-Ravez families in 1866.

The Johnstons greatly improved the property. They kept up with technical progress, surrounded themselves with highly competent staff, and called on excellent architects. The Victorian towers on each side of the Directoire facade were built during this era. In 1929 the property was acquired by Monsieur Desbarats-de-Burke, who sold it twelve

Facing page: winemaking, horizontal wine press, detail.

Château Ducru
Beaucaillou,
classified
in 1855.

Haut-Benauge
Citadel.

years later to Francis Borie. His grandchildren and their families are the current owners. The aptly named vineyard "*beaux cailloux*" (beautiful pebbles) is located on 50 hectares of beautiful gravelly outcrops running parallel to the Gironde, and belongs to the Saint-Julien AOC. A magnificent park with centuries-old trees extends towards the river*.

Great attention is paid to the wine, which receives constant and meticulous care. No detail is overlooked to produce the finest quality. Many specialists consider Ducru-Beaucaillou to be the quintessence of Bordeaux wines, and especially of the Médoc*.

■ Entre-deux-Mers & Entre-deux-Mers Haut-Benauge (A.O.C.)

Geographically, Entre-deux-Mers is bordered on the north by the Dordogne, on the south-west by the Garonne, and on the south-east by the administrative border of the Gironde department. Its plateaus and hillsides (where the tip of the department is to be found) are separated by the rivers and streams that criss-cross the region.

Entre-deux-Mers is a lovely region with a rich and magnificent historical, archeological, and monumental heritage: among its attractions are megalithic sites, mills, dovecots,

churches, abbeys, fortified towns, and old villages. Given the size of the region, the soil is very varied, ranging from *palus*, consisting of alluvium, by the river* to pure gravel requirements are identical to those of the Entre-deux-Mers AOC.

Red wines from this region are entitled only to the Bordeaux or Bordeaux Supérieur AOC*.

Château d'Escurac.

on some hillsides. On the plateaux, the soil is often silicious clay or clay-limestone and can be gravelly.

Today, the white wines of Entre-deux-Mers are exclusively dry. Most often made with Sauvignon, Sémillon and Muscadelle, they have a brilliant pale gold color. These are fruity, agreeably perfumed, refined, elegant, and flavorful wines. They are usually drunk young to appreciate their full fruit and vigor.

White wines from the towns of Targon, Ladaux, Soulignac, Cantois, Escoussans, Arbis, Saint-Pierre-de-Bat, Gornac, and Mourens can use the Entre-deux-Mers-Haut-Benauge AOC. Their production

■ Escurac (Ch. d')

Château Escurac's eleventh-century chapel displays evidence of the property's long winemaking tradition.

In 1839, a journal devoted to the special interests of the Gironde's wine-growing properties wrote of this *cru*: "From the time we started to classify the wines of the Gironde, we have considered those of M. Pépin d'Escurac to be a Médoc Fifth Growth; we will keep them there because in our opinion they deserve it, even if this overly timorous owner wished to be reduced to the category of good *bourgeois* wines..."

Even if the category of Fifth Growth at that time would

correspond to a Médoc Bourgeois Supérieur today, this opinion reveals the quality of Château Escurac's *terroir**. The vineyard is located on one of the highest hilltops of the Médoc and is characterized by a high proportion of deep gravel. Planted with a harmonious mix of the Médoc's main grape varieties, it is cultivated using the best techniques.

The owner has installed excellent equipment: a *cuvier* and storehouse for barrels. Under close supervision, the meeting of modern vinification techniques and traditional maturation gives the wine finesse, bouquet, and distinction.

▦ FRATERNITIES

In the Gironde, throughout France and abroad, fraternities organize exclusive gatherings which might seem quaint to some but which have an essential goal: to encourage consumers to discover and rediscover the region's many appellations, and to enhance the image of Bordeaux wine.

All the fraternities take part in group activities under the auspices of the *Grand Conseil du Vin de Bordeaux* (Great Council of Bordeaux Wine). Francis Fouquet, Grand Master and President of the Great Council, gives this definition of their role: "Certainly we wish to promote Bordeaux wines, but our thoughts run deeper: to bring together men and women who, across the world, share the same conceptions of education and quality of life."

There are nineteen wine fraternities in the Gironde, the oldest of which is the Jurade de Saint-Émilion, founded in 1948.

Château Laroque, *Grand Cru Classé*.

■ Fronsac & Canon-Fronsac (A.O.C.)

The Tertre de Fronsac, at the highest point of this area, has been inhabited for many centuries. Under Charlemagne, an impressive fortress was built, which long protected the locals from barbarian invasions. Henry IV made Fronsac the centre of his dukedom. On the ruins of the fortress, which was destroyed in 1623, the Duke of Richelieu—who was also Duke of Fronsac—built a charming Italian folly, where elegant, witty parties were held. As a result of these, many of the country's most important figures came to think highly of Fronsac's wines.

Because of their particularly favorable locations, their *terroir**, and a microclimate extremely well suited to wine-growing, six towns (Fronsac, La Rivière, Saint-Germain-la-Rivière, Saint-Michel-de-Fronsac, Saint-Aignan, and Saillans) plus some parts of Galgon benefit from

the specific Fronsac AOC. Certain parts of Fronsac and Saint-Michel de Fronsac are entitled to an even more specific AOC, Canon-Fronsac, though production conditions are identical in these areas.

The soil in the Fronsac region is very varied. Along the Dordogne and the Isle there is *palus*, consisting of alluvium; on the slopes and on hilltops, it is clay-limestone or clay-sand. The subsoil is generally limestone (starfish limestone), or clay-limestone.

Part of the Fronsac wine-growing region takes its name from the Côte de Canon. Among the soils found here is clay-limestone on a bed of starfish limestone. Canon-Fronsac wines owe their reputation, and their AOC, largely to the nature of this subsoil.

The AOC wines of Fronsac and Canon-Fronsac are essentially wines grown on hillsides. As a result of this, they have body and texture. They are richly and brilliantly colored, either

Fronsac vines in the mist.

vermilion red, or intense ruby. As they age, they sometimes take on a topaz tint, characteristic of wines from great limestone *terroirs**.

The nose is potent and elegant. Berry aromas develop, followed by notes of pepper, spices, and sometimes even truffle. In the mouth, these are full, rich, and supple wines. Names that stand out among the *crus* are Châteaux Canon, Haut-Mazeris, La Rivière, and Moulin Haut-Laroque*.

Girondins

The Girondins were the principal enemies of the Jacobins during the French Revolution. This independent spirit seems to be an inherent part of the south-western region of Gascony. The writers Montesquieu and Montaigne spring to mind, as does the image of Cyrano de Bergerac. The cultivation of the vine, which has shaped so much of the Gironde countryside, has perhaps also shaped the spirit of those who live with it and harvest its fruit. Whatever its source, this spirit goes back a long way: it is characteristic of this wine-growing region, and is one of the factors that has allowed it to become and remain the main wineproducing area in the world.

Grand Mouëys (Ch.)

Château Grand-Mouëys and the vast vineyard that surrounds it are located on a gravelly outcrop, most of which faces south or

Detail of Bacchus on the monument to the Girondins in Bordeaux, Place des Quinconces.

south-west. Its 170 uninterrupted hectares cover three hills of the Capian commune. The property, whose winemaking tradition goes back to Gallo-Roman times, belonged to the Templars during the Middle Ages.

In 1710, a branch of the Fesquet family—linked to the Chèze family, advisers to the King, and to the Barons of Capian—moved into the Piras residence, on the west side of the hill of the same name which figures on Belleyme's famous late eighteenth-century map. In 1880 Eugène Fabars and his son-in-law Count Charles de Langsdorff acquired this estate to extend the lands of Grand-Mouëys. In the nineteenth century, the enlarged property was sold at auction to the Grenouilleau family of Bordeaux merchants.

In 1989 the Bömers family, of the Bremen company of Reidemeister & Ulrichs, acquired the property and invested considerable sums in the vineyard and storehouses.

Twenty-one hectares of vineyards produce about 100 *tonneaux** of magnificent and distinguished white wine, some of which is aged in oak casks.

The red wine produced here is one of the best of the Premières Côtes de Bordeaux*. After having matured for eighteen months in oak casks (fifty percent new casks), the wine is bottled at the château.

CHÂTEAU
DU
GRAND MOUËYS
PREMIÈRES
CÔTES DE BORDEAUX
APPELLATION PREMIÈRES CÔTES DE BORDEAUX CONTRÔLÉE
S.C.A. LES TROIS COLLINES
PROPRIÉTAIRE À CAPIAN
GIRONDE - FRANCE
PRODUCE OF FRANCE
MIS EN BOUTEILLE AU CHÂTEAU

■ GRAVES & GRAVES SUPÉRIEURES (A.O.C.)

It is undoubtedly in this area, within and just outside the city of Bordeaux, that the region's winemaking roots run deepest. Graves wines, both red and white, have always increased the reputation of Bordeaux wines around the world. During the Middle Ages they were particularly renowned, and punishments were severe for those who cheated the public by passing off wines from other regions as being from Graves. Under the jurisdiction of Bordeaux, the vineyard at that time completely encircled the city. Until 1908, editions of the Féret guide listed vineyards in the city of Bordeaux under this appellation. Great names are attached to this historic region: Edward, the Black Prince owned a hunting lodge at Léognan; the philosopher-wine-grower Montesquieu spent time at Château de La Brède and Château Rochemorin; and Cardinal de Lamothe lived at Château Roquetaillade. The Graves region begins at the southern tip of the Médoc, extending for some sixty kilometers, with a width of fifteen to twenty kilometers. It is bordered on the east by alluvial plains along the Garonne and on the west by the Landes forest, which during one period began to encroach on the vineyards. As the name suggests, the soils and subsoils of this region consist mainly of pebbles, rocks, gravel of various sizes, and sand mixed with alluvium or clay, sometimes on a bed of rock but more often on pure sand or sand containing particles of iron. Because of its structure, this soil is very permeable. Though no geological formation, in the Bordeaux region or elsewhere, holds a unique claim to quality, Graves is ideal in many ways. Protected from rainstorms by the pine forest on the west and from excessive heat and humidity by breezes coming from the nearby Garonne, the Graves wine-growing area has an exceptional microclimate. Typified by the wines of such châteaux as Chantegrive, Floridère, du Grand-Bos, du Seuil*, de Portets, or of the Vieux Château Gaubert*, Graves wines have great finesse and aging potential whether they are red, white, or golden. Red Graves, shaped by their terroir*, are elegant and structured, refined and aromatic; their complexity comes from the infinite variety of soils and subsoils, and the personalities of the growers. With age, they develop aromas of spices, smoke, and very ripe fruit. The fruit of judicious blends of Sémillon, Sauvignon, and Muscadelle, white Graves are lively and structured, ample, perfumed, long, and flavorful, sometimes with a hint of oak from the cask. Only white wines are entitled to the Graves Supérieures AOC: these are sweet white wines of a beautiful golden color, sometimes with a touch of amber. Dense, round, and subtle, they have aromas of citrus and peach, with delicate notes of apricot, acacia, and honey in the mouth. One of this region's crus*, Château Haut-Brion, was classified a First Growth in 1855. Its fame no doubt had something to do with the Institut National des Appellations d'Origine's decision a few years ago to create a new AOC for Pessac-Léognan*.

Château de Landiras, nineteenth-century engraving.

CHÂTEAU
HAUT BRONDEAU
Graves de Vayres
APPELLATION GRAVES DE VAYRES CONTROLÉE
12,5% vol.   *1996*   750 ml e
SOCIÉTÉ CIVILE CHÂTEAU HAUT BRONDEAU
33800 ARVEYRES · GIRONDE · FRANCE
MIS EN BOUTEILLE AU CHÂTEAU
PRODUIT DE FRANCE

The red wines are delicate and refined, and can be enjoyed fairly young.

■ Guiraud (Ch.)

Château Guiraud, formerly the Château de Bayle, was classified in 1855. Along with the Château d'Yquem*, it is the only First Growth to be located in the Sauternes* commune.

Until the 1855 classification, the name Guiraud brought to mind a powerful family rather than a wine. This family, whose roots in the region went back to the seventeenth century, had a significant impact on Sauternes. But only since 1981, when the property was acquired by Canadian shipbuilder Frank Narby, has Guiraud regained the prestige, quality, and grandeur it deserves, given its fabulous *terroir**.

The property consists of 118 hectares, of which 100 are devoted to wine-growing.

Complementing the quality of the soils and of the vineyard are the best growing and harvesting techniques: the grapes are harvested bunch by bunch, so that only those affected by noble rot, or *Botrytis cinerea**, are picked.

Guiraud wine stands out for its generosity, elegance, perfect balance, and highly developed bouquet. With age it grows more refined while keeping its structure, and becomes extremely delicate.

■ Graves de Vayres (A.O.C.)

Near Libourne, the wine-growing region of Graves de Vayres is on the left bank of the Dordogne. It forms a relatively small area of gravelly soils in the vast region of Entre-deux-Mers*, in the Vayres commune, and on the Arveyres plateau.

The soils on which these wines are produced are generally clay-limestone, gravelly sand or clay-sand, on a gravelly or fairly compact clay-sand subsoil.

White wines of this region can be dry and distinctive thanks to the Sauvignon; they are sometimes sweet, supple, and generous thanks to the Sémillion, which is harvested over-ripe.

■ Haut-Brion (Ch.)

A great *cru* in the city. It was in the Graves region, very near Bordeaux but outside its walls, that Jean de Pontac created the wine-growing estate Château Haut-Brion in 1525. The north wing of the existing château was built in 1550. During the

1ᵉʳ CRU CLASSÉ   CLASSEMENT DE 1855

CHÂTEAU GUIRAUD
1ᵉʳ CRU
SAUTERNES
14% vol.   Appellation Sauternes Contrôlée   750 ml

1990

MIS EN BOUTEILLE AU CHÂTEAU

Product of France

S.C.A. DU CHÂTEAU GUIRAUD, PROPRIÉTAIRE À SAUTERNES (GIRONDE)

seventeenth and eighteenth centuries, his descendants applied patient technological research to produce a new type of wine, which became a model for great Bordeaux wines. These efforts allowed Arnaud de Pontac, as early as 1660, to identify and personalize his production. From this period onwards, the wines of Pontac and later Haut-Brion were hugely successful in London. Bordeaux's first great *cru* was born. The first to set the standard, Haut-Brion has maintained its reputation throughout its history, which also belongs to the history of Bordeaux and of France. Illustrious figures have left their mark on Haut-Brion: admirals, a bishop, a Marshal of France, a governor of Guyenne, three mayors of Bordeaux, Charles-Maurice de Talleyrand-Périgord while he was foreign minister for the Consulate and Empire, and more recently the American ambassador to Paris, Clarence Douglas Dillon, who was also the American minister of finance under John F. Kennedy. For nearly four centuries the owners and managers of Haut-Brion have been obsessed with maintaining the quality of its wines. A First Growth can never fall behind technologically, nor ever make mistakes. Honored with first place, it owes it to itself to hold on to the title. During the 1960s Haut-Brion was the first of the

great *crus* to innovate with new stainless steel fermentation vats; today it is the first to improve the grape varieties it uses by patient and laborious selection. Classified a Gironde First Growth in 1855, Château Haut-Brion became a Pessac-Léognan First Growth in 1973.

■ Haut-Marbuzet (Ch.)

In 1770 the vines of Marbuzet were part of the considerable inheritance that Sylvestre Fatin left to his two daughters, Pétronille and Rose. In 1825 the property was sold to the MacCarthy family, who were descendants of Irish Jacobites. In 1848, a bitter succession dispute led the MacCarthy family to sell the land in separate parcels. The Poissonier family acquired a seven-hectare parcel and named it Haut-Marbuzet. A hundred years later, in 1952, Hervé Duboscq bought the property under the *viager* system, paying a monthly sum until the death of its owner. Though without training in agriculture and oenology, he had a natural talent for viticulture. He succeeded in breathing life back into this vineyard, creating a wine with a distinctive style. In 1962 his son Henri joined him in working towards the only goal that counts for the Duboscq, which is Haut-Marbuzet's glory. After the acquisition of the neighboring vineyards which originally belonged to the MacCarthy family (Hautes Graves de Marbuzet, MacCarthy,

55

HAUT-MARBUZET

Château
Haut-Marbuzet.

Haut-Médoc.

Moula, Eyquem Marbuzet, Fontanelle, Hostein Marbuzet, Rose de Marbuzet, Lartigue), the property grew to fifty hectares by 1996.

This vineyard's excellence stems from its marvellous outcrop of Günz gravel with a clay-limestone subsoil which contains iron in its reduced form. Each vintage is matured in new Bordeaux oak casks*. These give the wine a perfumed smoothness that softens the traditional virility of Saint-Estèphe* wines. The wine is charming from the moment it is bottled, gaining in subtlety with age thanks to its magnificent *terroir*.

■ Haut-Médoc (A.O.C.)

Médoc and Haut-Médoc officially became separate appellations in 1935. This division, which confirmed a long-established custom, was due to where they are situated in relation to the Gironde: the Haut-Médoc is upstream, while the Bas-Médoc, known simply as the Médoc, is downstream.

The Haut-Médoc is a sixty-kilometer stretch of land along the left bank of the Garonne and the Gironde. Within this territory, aside from the six communal appellations—Margaux*, Moulis*, Listrac*, Saint-Julien*, Pauillac*, and Saint-Estèphe*—lie some remarkable wine-growing sites. These consist mainly of outcrops of very permeable Garonne gravel on a variety of subsoils.

The Haut-Médoc AOC consists of five *crus* classified in 1855, including Château Belgrave*. The bulk of the production comes from 140 *Crus Bourgeois*, including Châteaux Clément-Pichon, Paloumey, du Moulin Rouge, Lanessan, and Sociando Mallet, to name but a few.

Haut-Médoc AOC wines are lively and brilliant. Harmoniously balanced and generous without excess, they develop a remarkable bouquet over time. Depending on their origin they are more or less richly colored and powerful, but they all possess a distinctive Médoc character which accounts for their popularity throughout the world.

■ Investors

Large and small investors have always been drawn to Bordeaux wines, both by great interest and the potential for profit. They were bankers in the nineteenth century, insurers and heads of industry in the

twentieth. If the proportion of wine estates in their hands is not as high as it is said to be, it should be acknowledged that in many cases these investors have allowed major wine-growers to keep up with the latest technology, and also to hold on to estates they might have otherwise lost. In recent years no AOC has escaped this trend, which has contributed to the improvement in quality of Bordeaux wines.

Wine cellar of Château Pichon-Longueville.

■ Lalande-de-Pomerol (A.O.C.)

The Lalande-de-Pomerol AOC is reserved only for wines produced in the communes of Lalande-de-Pomerol and Néac. This region is located on one of the pilgrim paths that led to Saint James of Compostela. The Knights of Saint John of Jerusalem and the Knights of the Order of Malta built

The church at Néac.

refuges, hospices, and residences here. Dating from the twelfth century, the church of Lalande-de-Pomerol, the only one of its kind in Libourne, is the only remaining monument of the Hospitallers.

This region, in which vines have been cultivated since the tenth or eleventh century, extends west from Saint-Émilion*. The landscape grows less rugged towards the valley of the Isle river. The soil is clay and clay-gravel on the east, gravel on the north and north-east, and increasingly sandy towards the west. Near the point where the Dordogne and the Isle converge, Lalande-de-Pomerol shares the sunny, hot, and humid climate of its neighboring AOCs (Saint-Émilion*, Pomerol*, Fronsac*), which is perfect for wine-growing.

Lalande-de-Pomerol AOCs are generally richly colored, velvety, powerful, and perfumed, with great finesse thanks to the harmonious blend of grape varieties. The range is quite varied depending on the soils and sub-soils in which the vines were cultivated. A few *crus* that demonstrate this diversity are Châteaux Perron, de Viaud, Haut Chaigneau, Grand Ormeau, and le Clos de l'Eglise.

■ Latour (Ch.)

The Château Latour vineyard, created around 1680, is one of the oldest in the Médoc.

Thanks to the work of the Marquis de Ségur, its owner in the early eighteenth century, the vineyard very quickly acquired an outstanding reputation for the quality of its wines. These benefit from exceptional geological conditions on gravelly outcrops overlooking the Gironde, closer to the river* than any other vineyard in the Médoc.

The heart of the vineyard, the Enclos, consists of forty-seven hectares of old vines which are carefully looked after, as only they can produce the great wine of Pauillac*. This vineyard is planted with seventy-eight percent Cabernet Sauvignon and seventeen percent Merlot, with the remaining five percent divided between Cabernet Franc and Petit Verdot.

The eighteen hectares of land that are outside the Enclos, and vines less than ten years old, that fall just short of the AOC requirements, produce the property's second wine, Les Forts de Latour.

In 1963 the vineyard's acquisition by the British group Pearson gave a strong boost to this First Growth, allowing it to invest in the latest technology: this is how Latour, in 1964, became one of the first estates to purchase temperature-controlled stainless steel vats for winemaking.

Wines are matured in the traditional way in new Bordeaux oak casks* for seventeen to twenty months. This happy marriage of progress and tradition has allowed Latour to attain a supreme quality.

After thirty years of "English occupation," Château Latour became French once more when it was bought by François Pinault in June 1993.

Château Latour, a First Growth classified in 1855.

59

■ Latour Martillac (Ch.)

This château owes its name to the tower in its main courtyard: the staircase of a small fort, built in the twelfth century by Montesquieu's ancestors. Its ruins were probably used to build the noble, horseshoe-shaped residence, of which only the central charterhouse today remains.

Alfred Kressmann, who bought this Château Latour in 1929, changed the name both to avoid confusion with the illustrious Médoc château of the same name and to honor the village where his father, Édouard, had started a wine-shipping business in 1871.

One parcel of land, planted with vines in 1884, is a living proof of this interest: it still contains all the grape varieties that Édouard Kressmann selected to give his "Graves Monopole Dry"—named by the diva Adelina Patti in 1892—the breed, nerve, and fruit which, enhanced by the great age of these irreplaceable vines, characterize this Pessac-Léognan *cru*.

Alfred wasted no time in restructuring the vineyard, which had been reduced to twelve hectares, eight of which were used to produce white wine, the remaining four to make red. Without touching the oldest parcels, he inverted the proportion by adding Cabernet Sauvignon to the existing Merlot, Malbec, and Petit-Verdot. After being interrupted by World War II, the work was continued by his son Jean, who became the property's manager in 1940, and inherited it in 1954. Jean realized Alfred's dream by

Château Latour Martillac, a Graves *cru* classified for its reds and whites.

A Listrac vineyard.

buying the gravelly plateau that separated the property from the village and gradually increased the vineyard to thirty-eight hectares: twenty-eight for red wine and ten for white.

A Graves Classified Growth for its reds and whites, this property has belonged since 1974 to a

family-owned agricultural real estate company run by Loïc and Tristan Kressmann.

■ Listrac-Médoc (A.O.C.)

Monsieur d'Armailhac, in his 1855 book on viticulture in the Médoc, said the Listrac plateau could be compared to the region's most favorably placed properties. With magnificent outcrops on either side—Forréad to the south and Fourcas to the north—the five-kilometer-long Listrac plateau is one of the highest in the Médoc.

Monsieur Boissenot, a wine specialist, describes Listrac wine as follows: "Listrac wine presents in the mouth an extraordinary body, enveloping the palate. Its presence is built. This is the wine of oenophiles, this is the wine that you chew, so tight is its texture. Solidly constituted, tannic and structured, it is the perfect meeting of the fruit provided by Cabernet and the strength supplied by Merlot. As a result it is ample and silky, a mixture of spirit and virility."

Wine-lovers will encounter this style by tasting wines from châteaux such as Fourcas-Dupré, Fourcas-Hosten, or

Saransot-Dupré, La Lausette, Peyredon la Gravette, and Clarke.

■ Loupiac (A.O.C.)

Located at the foot of the hills, the town of Loupiac has sometimes suffered from the Garonne river's caprices. The vines, however, benefit from the southern exposure of hillsides which are often quite steep. Vines have grown in this region since the end of the thirteenth century. As in Sainte-Croix-du-Mont*, the land is rugged and the soil is clay-limestone, or clay-sand towards the east.

Loupiac's white wine has a sweetness, fruit, and vigor that can satisfy the most demanding and delicate of palates. Refined, firm, and generous, it gains in quality as it ages. The quality of each *cru* depends, naturally, on the nature of its *terroir**. Even more important is the care the wine-grower takes in cultivation and especially during the harvest and vinification. Châteaux Mémoires, de Ricaud,

Vines at
Loupiac.

du Cros, and Clos Jean are out-standing examples of this care-ful attention.

Red wine produced in the Lou-piac appellation* is entitled only to the Bordeaux Supérieur* or Bordeaux* AOC, though it is located within the area of the Premières Côtes de Bordeaux* appellation.

■ Lussac-Saint-Émilion (A.O.C.)

Well before the Christian era and Gallo-Roman civilization, pagan rites were celebrated here: as is proved by a Gallic megalith at the Tertre de Picampeau. Either legend or history has it that a person named Lucius or Lucciacus planted the first vines on the surrounding hills during the Gallo-Roman period.

This property, Lucianus, is said to have given its name and boundaries to the Lussac parish. Pruning knives and amphoras, found by archeologists during deep excavations carried out here, confirm this belief.

Lussac-Saint-Émilion.

Well drained and well sited, the wine-growing *terroir** of Lussac-Saint-Emilion is perfectly suited to the production of quality red wines, as châteaux such as Bellevue, de Croix-Rambeau, and de la Grenière prove.

These wines are characterized by their deep color and their subtle nose, all finesse and generosity.

Just like the people who produce them, they are excellent dining companions. Younger vintages get along marvellously with gutsy foods such as grilled red meats and game.

Then, as they age and mature, they go very well with roast meat and sauces.

■ Maison Blanche (Ch.)

Château Maison Blanche is a magnificent property of forty undivided hectares. Since the addition of the Lamarsalle vineyard—which also belonged to Lord Corbin's domain—at the beginning of the twentieth century, this has become one of the biggest and most beautiful estates of the Saint-Émilion region.

It is located a few acres from the meeting point of the appellations Lalande-de-Pomerol*, Pomerol*, Saint-Émilion*, and Montagne-Saint-Émilion*, and covers part of the lands of the ancient Gallo-Roman villa Lucianus.

The division of Roze Gruignet de Lobory's estate on May 2, 1765 showed that a vineyard existed at that time on the land of today's Château Maison Blanche.

Considered one of the best *crus* of the Montagne-Saint-Émilion* since the early 1900s, this wine is known throughout the world thanks to its distribution on all five continents.

Merlot and Cabernet vines produce about 190 *tonneaux** on clay hillsides and rocky plateaux. Only 80 of these will be separated, blended, matured in oak barrels, and bottled with the name Château Maison Blanche.

The property's second wine is marketed under the name Les Piliers de Maison-Blanche. Since the 1985 vintage, a limited edition wine has been produced using the techniques of the *Premiers Grands Crus*. This wine is marketed under the brand name of Louis Rapin.

MISE EN BOUTEILLES DU CHATEAU

Château Maison Blanche

ＭＯＮＴＡＧＮＥ-ＳＡＩＮＴ-ＥＭＩＬＩＯＮ

1959

APPELLATION MONTAGNE-S-ÉMILION CONTROLÉE

LOUIS RAPIN PROPRIÉTAIRE A MONTAGNE (GIRONDE)

◼ Margaux (A.O.C.)

As is the case with most of the vineyards around the city of Bordeaux, vines were planted in the Margaux region in Gallo-Roman times.

If a text referred to Château Margaux at the beginning of the eighteenth century, it was not until the end of that century that the owners became aware of the value of their lands and the wine's aging potential. It is interesting to note that it was not until a century after the 1855 classification that the communes won their long battle to have a precisely defined Margaux AOC.

The Margaux vineyard rests mainly on a layers of soil deposited by a river during the Quaternary era. These form a vast plateau, about six kilometers long and two kilometers wide, surrounded by gravelly outcrops. Mixed with medium-sized shingle, this is one of the best examples of Günz gravel in the Haut-Médoc. Beneath it lies an underlayer of limestone or clayey marl from the Tertiary era. Well protected from ocean winds by the forest, this *terroir** benefits from cool breezes from the Gironde which temper the climate.

All the conditions for great wine are present: poor soils combined with permeable gravel, and gently sloping outcrops.

Between them, the five communes of the Margaux AOC have twenty-one growths classified in 1855, including one First Growth, Châteaux Margaux. Also worth a special mention is Château Palmer, which has benefited from the investments of the Pereire brothers. A few *Crus Bourgeois* are also worthy representatives of the AOC, notably Châteaux Deyrem Valentin, d'Angludet, and Monbrison.

Margaux AOC wines have a lovely ruby color, a great deal of finesse, and a characteristic nose. They are generous without being overwhelming. When the vinification has been successful, many connoisseurs consider Margaux to be one of the best wines in the world. Whatever its origin and classification—*Classé, Bourgeois, Artisan,* or other—Margaux wine offers an exceptional and infinite palette of fruity tastes. Its character is elegant, subtle, and full. Margaux is often considered to be the most feminine wine of the Médoc because of its delicacy, suppleness, and fruity aromas—perhaps this is why it keeps all these qualities for so long.

Hand-picking grapes in the Médoc.

■ MARGAUX (CH.)

With its Ionic peristyle, monumental staircase and classic facade, Château Margaux is as imposing as the celebrated *cru* of the same name. Nobility of balance and size, and a sumptuous style aptly define both this architectural jewel and the wine produced by the vineyards that surround it. This distinguished residence housed Edward III, King of England; at the time it was one of the most imposing fortified châteaux in Guyenne. In the twelfth century, when it was known as La Mothe, it was owned by the powerful Albret family. Later it belonged to the Montferrand family, then to the Lords of Durfort. In the mid-eighteenth century Château Margaux became the property of Monsieur de Fumel, a Bordeaux military commander who played a large part in building this magnificent estate's reputation. When the Marquis de la Colonilla acquired the property in 1802 he had the gothic manor house torn down and ordered the construction of the present château. This was designed by the architect Louis Combes, a student of Victor Louis, and is still much admired. Count Pillet-Will, who took over the property in 1879, also contributed to the vineyard's fame. The château and its 260 hectares of vineyards now belong to the Château Margaux SCA. The future of this First Growth, classified in 1855, is now in the hands of Corinne Mentzelopoulos. Though its size is impressive, this vineyard is cultivated with attention to the smallest detail and dedication to quality. Only rigorously selected wines have the honor of bearing the Châteaux Margaux label. As a result of this strict selection, a second wine is now produced with the label Pavillon Rouge du Château Margaux. The quality is comparable, but this wine is ready to drink much earlier.

For more than a century a small area of about twelve hectares of fine gravel has been reserved for growing Sauvignon Blanc. This produces a small quantity of dry, original, and subtle white wine, the Pavillon Blanc du Château Margaux.

Château Margaux, a First Growth classified in 1855.

■ MÉDOC (A.O.C.)

Geographically, the Médoc is the long triangular peninsula that stretches from the Jalle (stream) of Blanquefort north-west of Bordeaux to the tip of Graves, between the Atlantic Ocean on the west and the Gironde river on the east.

The vineyard itself, however, occupies a much smaller area, almost all of which follows the banks of the river* between Blanquefort in the south and Saint-Vivien-de-Médoc to the north. On the west the vineyard is bordered by the pine forest facing the Atlantic, which protects the vines from the ocean winds. Because of the frosts that the forest attracts, which stop the vines from growing, from time to time the vineyard has been reduced in size.

Established along the estuary of the Gironde, the Médoc wine-growing region occupies a favored and practically unique position. The vineyard is sandwiched between two major bodies of water, the ocean and the estuary, which create one of the best possible microclimates: small variations in temperature and a reasonable amount of humidity which, combined with the heat and sunlight, are particularly beneficial to the grapes when they are ripening.

The vines grow on a succession of gravelly ridges (Günz gravel), the remains of ancient alluvium deposited by glaciers from the Pyrenees and the Massif Central, which have been broken up as they were eroded by the river.

This gravelly soil is poor and ill-suited to any cultivation but vines and forests. However, because of its permeability, it is ideal for producing quality wines—the vine roots have to penetrate deeply into the soil to find water and other elements essential to their development.

The quality of wines produced in the Médoc varies according to the percentage of each grape variety used: Cabernet Sauvignon, Cabernet Franc, Merlot, and Petit-Verdot. According to the definition of the Médoc AOC, this appellation covers all the *terroirs** and wine-growing communes of the Médoc peninsula, including those of the Haut-Médoc AOC.

In reality, though, Médoc AOC wines are produced mainly by the communes to the north and north-west of Saint-Seurin-de-Cadourne, such as those of Châteaux Tour Haut-Caussan*, d'Escurac*, les Ormes Sorbet, Potensac, Patache d'Aux, and Tour-de-By.

Médoc AOC wines are enchanting in more ways than one. The variety of soils, the proportion of grape varieties used (Cabernet Sauvignon, Cabernet Franc, Merlot, and Petit-Verdot) and the individual styles of the winemakers result in wines which, despite a family resemblance, have their own personalities and qualities, which makes them all the more charming.

Wine-lovers will find in Médoc an infinite range of sensations and pleasures for all the senses.

An expanse of vines in the Médoc region stretching as far as the eye can see.

■ Mondésir Gazin (Ch.)

Monsieur Pasquet bought this vineyard in 1990 and was able to draw on his previous experience working in Saint-Estèphe* on the vineyards of Château Marbuzet*—a useful apprenticeship.

When M. Pasquet acquired the vineyard, which produces a Premières Côtes de Blaye* AOC *cru*, it was already in excellent condition, with the vines averaging twenty-five years in age. His first projects were to restore the stones of the *longère* —a long building typical of the region— to their original blond beauty, and to bring the cellar up to his standards. For the winemaking, a sorting facility was added so that only perfectly sound grapes would go into the vats.

GRAND VIN DE BORDEAUX
CUVÉE PRESTIGE

CHATEAU
MONDESIR-GAZIN

PREMIERES COTES DE BLAYE
Appellation Premières Côtes de Blaye Contrôlée

1998

MARC PASQUET
VITICULTEUR A PLASSAC
GIRONDE FRANCE
13% vol.   75 cl

MIS EN BOUTEILLE AU CHÂTEAU
PRODUCE OF FRANCE

■ Montagne-Saint-Émilion (A.O.C.)

With a privileged location in the heart of the Saint-Émilion region, Montagne is a commune with a rich history, but it deserves attention as much for its wine production and its inhabitants' deep-seated attachment to their *terroir** as for its past and its sights. So strong is its attachment to wine that the commune boasts a Maison du Vin, a Musée du Vigneron Paysan (Museum of the Country Wine-Grower), and the agricultural college of Libourne-Montagne, one of the best in France for training in wine-growing and winemaking, and for higher level wine studies. Montagne's soil is similar to that of the Saint-Émilion appellation*. The hills are generally limestone or clay-limestone on a subsoil of starfish limestone.

Also on the hillsides and plateaus are found siliceous-clay soil, and subsoils that sometimes have an iron content.

Like its celebrated neighbor Saint-Émilion, there is not one, but rather many Montagne-Saint-Émilion wines. All of them are delightful, to a greater or lesser degree—especially enjoyable are those of Châteaux Maison-Blanche*, Faizeau, Montaiguillon, Calon, and Petit-Clos du Roy.

Depending on their origin, their color is lighter or darker and ranges from cherry to vermilion or ruby, or even purple. The nose can be fresh, lively, floral, powerful, and rich, but is always suave. In the mouth they can be more or less tannic, but they always express their pedigree with smoothness, generosity, and distinction. Recent vintages go well with any food; older wines reveal their richness, bouquet, and strength with game, poultry, and sauces.

■ Montrose (Ch.)

The land of Château Montrose was sold by a ruling of the Bordeaux parliament to Etienne Théodore Dumoulin by Alexandre de Ségur on March 6, 1778. At the time, this gravelly hill of more than eighty hectares was a heather-covered moor. Dumoulin started to have the château built in 1815, and he planted the vineyard at the same time. In 1825 only five to six hectares of vines had been planted, but by 1832 there were 35 hectares. In 1855 Château Montrose was classified a Second Growth. At that time, it produced 100–150 *tonneaux** of wine. It remained in the hands of the Dumoulin family until 1866, when Mathieu Dollfus bought it for 500,000 francs. Dollfus did some rebuilding and enlarged the vineyard. By 1880, it covered 65 hectares and produced 200–250 *tonneaux*. When Dollfus died his heirs sold the property to Jean Hostein for 1,500,000 francs. A few years later, Hostein sold it to his son-in-law, Louis Charmolüe, whose

Aerial view of Montagne-Saint-Émilion.

Château Montrose, classified in 1855.

family has owned the property ever since.

The estate is remarkably well arranged. The vineyard, which has only one tenant, is divided into big squares separated by broad alleys, which are planted with selected grape varieties such as Cabernet Franc, Cabernet Sauvignon, and Merlot. This is why the Château Montrose *Grand Cru* is considered a model vineyard. The property also owes its great reputation to its gravelly soil and to its unusual exposure. Connoisseurs rank the wine as one of the best of its category, a favored status which seems justified given its consistently high quality. Those in the know say Montrose is the "Latour of Saint-Estèphe," which hardly seems an exaggeration.

■ Moulin Haut-Laroque (Ch.)

This *cru* is an example of a family-run vineyard. The property of the Hervé family for many generations, it took its present form at the end of the nineteenth century. The fifteen hectares of vines in the Saillans commune, part of the Fronsac AOC, are particularly well positioned. Jean-Noël Hervé, who has a great respect for tradition, has devoted himself since 1977 to bringing out the best in this outstanding *terroir**, and to producing wines typical of the appellation.

■ Moulis or Moulis-en-Médoc (A.O.C.)

The name of this commune is no doubt due to the many mills—both water and wind—once found on its land. Moulis is thus a corruption of the Latin words *molinis* and *mola*. If the name points to the fact that grain crops were grown here, it is also known that vines were planted by some landowners and by a significant religious community during the Middle Ages.

The vineyard spread and established its reputation along with those of neighboring wine-growing communities, especially during the eighteenth and nineteenth centuries.

Due to the complexity of its land, rigorously selected for its crucial influence on the quality of the wines, Moulis-en-Médoc brings together an exceptional collection of Médoc wines and crus*.

More than ninety percent of the production comes from prestigious *Crus Bourgeois*, such as Chasse-Spleen, Poujeaux*, Maucaillou, Anthonic, Moulin à Vent, and Brillette. In the annual ranking of the Coupe des Crus Bourgeois du Médoc, a Moulis *cru* often comes first, second or third.

Producers can equally use the terms "appellation Moulis contrôlée" or "appellation Moulis-en-Médoc contrôlée" on their labels, but in no way does the choice of term imply that one wine is of superior quality or flavor to another.

Moulis and Moulis-en-Médoc wines display finesse, elegance, generosity, charm, and vigor. Their ruby color is intense and deep, and their bouquet elegant, with complex and powerful nuances.

Some specialists have said that the Moulis' *terroir*** is a remarkable concentration of the Médoc. The same can be said of its production. Wines that come from gravelly soils bring to mind the finesse of Margaux*, and the power and complexity of Saint-Julien*. The more robust wines from clay-limestone soils evoke the nobility of Pauillac*. They are ready to drink after eight or ten years; their tannin content allows them to continue to age gracefully.

Château Chasse Spleen.

■ Mouton Rothschild (Ch.)

In 1853, Baron Nathaniel de Rothschild, of the English side of the famous family, bought the Château Brane-Mouton and baptised the castle Château Mouton-Rothschild. Despite the excellence of this Pauillac* *cru*, no-one in the family took a real interest until 1922. That year, the twenty-year-old Baron Philippe, seduced by the charm of the property and its surroundings, decided to make it his life's work. In 1924, he initiated compulsory château bottling, which was practically unheard of at the time. In 1926, he added the famous, 100-metre-long Grand Chai, designed by the architect Charles Siclis.

In 1945, to celebrate the Liberation, Baron Philippe had the original idea of adding an appropriate drawing to the label of that vintage. It was a "V" for Victory and the first of a fascinating collection of original artworks created each year by famous painters, such as Chagall, Braque, Picasso, Warhol, or Delvaux, for Mouton labels. In 1962 he inaugurated the Musée du Vin dans l'Art (Museum of Wine in Art), which brought together three millennia of precious objects relating to vines and wine. Mouton thus became a major tourist* attraction, with thousands of visitors each year.

In 1973, after a long battle, Baron Philippe succeeded in having the 1855 classification revised and Mouton officially became a Médoc *Premier Cru Classé*.

After the death of Baron Philippe de Rothschild in 1988, his daughter, Baroness Philippine, who had worked closely with her father for several years, took over the running of the vineyard. Since then she has devoted herself to increase continually the quality and fame of this great wine whose motto proudly proclaims: "First I am, second I was, Mouton never changes."

■ Nodoz (Ch.)

This property goes back a long way: Count de Nodoz sold it in 1791 to the family of J.J. Bordes, a well-known merchant-shipowner in Bordeaux. This family improved the vineyard and established its reputation. During the wine-growing crisis of 1930, the Magdeleine family bought the property from the wine merchants Posso and Rosenfeld.

Beautifully located on a gravelly hillside, the vineyard covers forty hectares in the communes of Tauriac and Lansac. It benefits from maximum sunshine thanks to its east-south-east and south-west exposure.

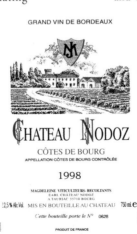

After a traditional vinification, Château Nodoz wines are matured in Bordeaux oak casks* for twelve to eighteen months, depending on the vintage.

The Côtes de Bourg* AOC wine has been rewarded with several medals in wine competitions and high praise in specialist magazines. A robust and generous wine, it can be enjoyed young but also offers surprises to those who are willing to wait.

■ Pauillac (A.O.C.)

From ancient times to the early twentieth century Pauillac was a thriving port thanks to its location halfway between the city of Bordeaux and the mouth of the Gironde. Many ships stopped here before heading towards Bordeaux or out to sea. Today, because the means of transport have changed, "all that remains is the evidence and the memory," as Bernard Ginestet wrote in his book on Pauillac wines.

Vines have grown here since the end of the Middle Ages, and spread bit by bit during the centuries that followed. But it was the creation of major estates in the early seventeenth, then the eighteenth and nineteenth centuries, that gave the region its current renown.

The soil of this AOC is made up of gravelly outcrops in the north and south, partly separated by the Pibran marsh. Their remarkable contours distinguish this *terroir** of Garonne gravel, which is fairly sandy and, therefore, well drained.

This commune contains eighteen classified growths, more than any other appellation. Among these are three First Growths: Lafite Rothschild, Latour*, and Mouton Rothschild* (classified in 1973). These eighteen *crus** account for eighty-four percent of the Pauillac AOC production!

Pauillac wines are among the most famous of the Médoc. They are powerful, intensely fruity, refined, and distinguished. Potent in their youth, the berry and flower aromas (blackcurrant, raspberry, violet, rose, iris) soften with time to a delicate bouquet. Rich and complex, the wines age particularly well. True gourmets like to postpone the pleasure of drinking them, and are richly rewarded.

Château Lafite, a First Growth classified in 1855, nineteenth century engraving.

■ PESSAC-LÉOGNAN (A.O.C.)

This is Bordeaux's newest AOC. Because the vineyards are located within Graves*, wines produced here can also be labelled with any of the region's AOCs.

Seeing their region threatened by urbanization, Pessac Léognan's producers worked with great perseverence to obtain a specific AOC. A number of factors made this a logical step. In this part of Graves, with remarkable consistency, the soil is particularly gravelly and typical of the region. The wines stand out by their quality—confirmed by fifteen editions of the Féret guide and their soaring prices. Historically, as one of the first Bordeaux vineyards, Pessac-Léognan also deserved recognition.

Today, about sixty crus* share this magnificent terroir*, including sixteen classified growths. Some of these are classified for their red wine: Château Haut-Brion* (classified a First Growth in 1855), but also Château Pape-Clément in Pessac, created in 1300 by Bertrand de Goth, who became Pope Clément V in 1305. Others are classified for their white wine, such as Couhins, or for both red and

Château Haut-Brion, a First Growth classified in 1855.

white, such as Domaine de Chevalier and Château Latour-Martillac*. This last vineyard is currently spreading onto building land in Bordeaux's urban zone, as is Domaine du Luchey, which will have its first harvest in 2001 after having disappeared for more than half a century. Also worth a mention among the best-known *crus* are Châteaux La Louvière, de Rouillac, de Grandmaison, Baret, and La Garde.

Red Pessac-Léognan AOC wines are particularly expressive. They have distinctive fruit, remarkable structure, and great finesse. Generally matured in oak casks, they will keep for a long time—the first sign of a high-quality wine. They are worth waiting for, and deserve to be drunk with respect.

White Pessac-Léognan wines, produced mainly with Sauvignon and Sémillon, are Bordeaux's best-known dry white wines. They owe this reputation not only to the richness of their aromatic palette, but also to their capacity for aging. Matured in oak casks, they can be amazingly fresh and lively after five, ten, or even twenty years.

■ Pétrus (Ch.)

Dominating the commune, as much by its position as by the quality of its wines, Château Pétrus produces a generous wine which is refined, rich, and perfumed, with a definite truffle aroma. These special qualities are due to its sandy-clay subsoil on an iron-rich base known as *crasse de fer*, which gives the wine its universally appreciated distinction. Madame E. Loubat took meticulous care of this beautiful vineyard, devoting equal attention to the viticulture and vinification. Since her death, her family has carried on the family tradition. Her aim is to preserve the wine's long-standing reputation around the world as the greatest Pomerol *cru**.

■ Pomerol (A.O.C.)

In the twelfth century, the powerful Hospitallers of Saint John of Jerusalem established their first Libournais Commanderie in the Pomerol commune. Here they built a manor, a hospital for pilgrims on their way to Saint James of Compostela, and a church.

Though the vineyard was virtually abandoned and devastated during the Hundred Years' War and the English occupation, it was re-established during the fifteenth and sixteenth centuries. The vineyard again suffered during the Wars of Religion. From 1900, though, Pomerol's wine-growers created a union to defend their appellation. One of their main objectives was to prevent wine-growers in neighboring communes from abusing the Pomerol name by stamping it on their casks.

Henri Enjalbert, in his book *The Great wines of Saint-Émilion, Pomerol and Fronsac*, helps his readers to understand the unique character of Pomerol's *terroir**. This region is blessed with an ideal microclimate and exceptional geographical conditions: compact or sandy gravel on the surface and a subsoil containing iron oxide.

No official classification exists in Pomerol, but there is an accepted ranking led by Château Pétrus. The order is not fixed—Pomerol's producers have a healthy spirit of competition which can only be beneficial to the AOC. With *crus* such as Vieux-Château-Certan, La Conseillante, Nénin, La Pointe, Clos René, de Sales, and Vieux Maillet to choose from, wine-lovers are spoiled for choice.

Pomerol wine can surprise those who taste it for the first time: it brings together the finesse of the Médoc* and the generosity of Saint-Émilion*. It is this combination of qualities that gives the wine its character. After aging* for a few years it reveals all its splendor and demands the full attention of nearly all the senses: sight for its brilliant, velvety, and dense color; smell for its exquisite and subtle aromas of small berries, truffle, and violet; taste combined with touch when in the mouth it unveils its silky body and the roundness of its flesh.

■ Poujeaux (Ch.)

In the sixteenth century Château Poujeaux belonged, under the name Salle de Poujeaux, to

Gaston de l'Isle. It was on the property of Tour Saint-Mambert (now known as Château Latour*). Renamed Château Poujeaux, it belonged to the Castaing family until the death of Philippe Castaing in 1920, when it became the property of François Theil. The name of his son, Jean Theil, has appeared on each vintage since 1947. Jean Theil used all his talent to unite the three Châteaux Poujeaux, and to re-establish

Decanting wine from an oak cask.

the single property that existed before 1880. When he died in 1981, two of his sons, Philippe and François, took over this Moulis* *Cru Bourgeois*. The latest equipment is used for the vinification. Maceration time varies from four to six weeks and the new wine is matured in Bordeaux oak casks*, half of which are renewed each year. Château Poujeaux belongs to the Bordeaux Wine Academy* and the Union des Grands Crus*.

79

■ PREMIÈRES CÔTES DE BORDEAUX (A.O.C.)

The Premières Côtes de Bordeaux region stretches from Bassens to Saint-Maixant along the entire length of the Garonne, following the river's twists and turns.

This hilly region makes for pleasant walking, offering many viewpoints. Visitors will also come across a number of small châteaux, monuments, and historic sites, such as the fortified towns of Rions and Cadillac*. Many famous people were born, lived or spent holidays in this area, including Rosa Bonheur, Henri de Toulouse-Lautrec, Anatole France, François Mauriac, and Gustave Eiffel. Today, many families have a holiday home in the region, and increasing numbers of people from abroad retire here, particularly from Britain and the Netherlands.

Vines grow on the slopes and hilltops along the river*; the vineyard consists of thirty-seven communes whose bell towers seem to mark the borders of the area.

Until recently, the northern part of this region was especially well-known and appreciated for its red wine production, while the southern part, whose microclimate aids the production of sweet white wines, was known for its whites. Both the reds and whites were noted for their quality, the result of a favored terroir*. They also benefited from their proximity to the city of Bordeaux and its policy of protectionism which lasted from the Middle Ages to the eighteenth century. During the nineteenth century these wines were sought out for their

Vineyards of the Premières Côtes,
Langoiran citadel.

ability to travel without deteriorating. Red wines of the Premières Côtes de Bordeaux are generally richly colored, well structured, and quite full-bodied. A high proportion of Merlot gives them roundness and supple tannins*; the freshness of their fruit can be enjoyed when they are drunk young. Thanks to their

solid structure, however, they express more delicacy and generosity as they age.

The white wines are sweet and can sometimes even be syrupy, when they are produced in the communes defined by the Cadillac* AOC. They are remarkable for their body and finesse. Produced mainly with Sémillon grapes, which gives them flavors of toast and candied fruits, these are fat, generous wines. The name of the commune where the grapes were grown can legally be added to the Premières Côtes de Bordeaux AOC. However, it is worth noting that in practice this is never done.

There are many worthwhile, enterprising estates in the Premières Côtes de Bordeaux. Among the best-known of these are Châteaux Reynon, de Birot, Nénine, du Grand Mouëys, de Marsan, de Plassan, de Haux, and de Manos.

◼ PRIMEUR

The *primeur* (young) wine market plays two essential roles in the Bordeaux wine trade. It is an important means of discovering the quality of the new wine, but above all, for classified growths and other sought-after wines, it covers the financial cost of storing the most recent vintage for an eighteen to twenty-four-month maturation period.

This trade is, by nature, mainly professional: growers negotiate with merchants*, using brokers* as middle-men. The wines then become available to the public through retailers and a few specialized wine merchants. The first stage determines the demand for that vintage and is a good way of predicting its success on the national and international wine markets.

Those who buy wine *en primeur* are gambling on its increase in value. Two factors come into play: the quality of future vintages and the international demand. Though the demand can be predicted with some accuracy, no-one can foresee the quality of the forthcoming vintage. In this sense, future vintages remain enigmatic. One thing is certain, though: in real terms, wine-lovers rarely lose money by regularly investing in the latest vintage.

■ Puisseguin-Saint-Émilion (A.O.C.)

Perched on a natural hill, the Puisseguin commune owes its name to the word *puy*, meaning mount, and Séguin, one of Charlemagne's lieutenants who had a château built on this strategic site.

It was during the eighteenth century that Puisseguin's economy began to rely largely on wine-growing and winemaking. Pierre Combret, a pioneer in wine-growing agronomy, introduced the use of grape varieties known as "noble" and made the most of this *terroir's* qualities. Many others followed suit. The commune's future was thus assured and Puisseguin earned its place in Bordeaux wine-growing history.

Situated at an altitude of 89 meters, Puisseguin's vineyards enjoy a mainly south-south-east exposure and a dry, bright, almost Mediterranean microclimate—proved by the presence of many holm oaks. Its hilly terrain of clay-limestone soil on a rocky subsoil provides good drainage and allows the vines to develop deep roots which draw out elements essential to the plants' development.

Nearly eighty properties make up this appellation*, including Châteaux Teillac, Guibeau-la-Fourvieille, Roc de Bernon, and Grand-Rigaud.

The richly colored wines of Puisseguin-Saint-Émilion are characterized by their structure, their strength, and a finesse which allows them to age beautifully and develop an ever more seductive bouquet.

If they are given enough air (decanted), these wines can be enjoyed young with strongly flavored foods, which they complement well. Later, at the peak of their maturity, they make the perfect counterpoint to white meats and subtle sauces.

The Millésima cellars.

A Puisseguin vineyard.

■ Puygueraud (Ch.)

Georges Thienpoint bought Château Puygueraud in 1946. The poor state of the vineyard forced him to rip out all the vines and turn the property into farmland for nearly thirty years, restructuring and regenerating the soil. At the end of the 1970s, when he decided to replant the vineyard, the quality of the soil allowed him to use low-yield rootstock. He chose the plants carefully and spaced them according to the specific

meaning that it takes place alternately in stainless steel vats and oak casks (25 percent new each year) whose contents are changed during frequent racking (drawing the juice off the lees).

Puygueraud wines, which have been granted the Bordeaux Côtes de Francs* AOC, are well structured. A high proportion of Cabernet gives them subtlety and elegance. These are long-lived, distinctive wines with a rich and complex nose.

■ Rame (Ch. la)

During the French Revolution, La Rame belonged to Baron de Vertheuil, governor of the Ile d'Oléron off the west coast of France, and Lord of Rame. One of the oldest and best-known Bordeaux *crus*, La Rame was already considered one of the leading *crus* of its AOC by the Bordeaux wine trade in the nineteenth century. The Armand family, who had lived in Sainte-Croix-du-Mont* for more than a century, bought this estate in 1956, when disastrous frosts struck the Bordeaux vineyards. Aware of the land's potential, Clause Armand used all his means to restore it. By 1969 he was finally able to renovate the cellars. La Rame

qualities of the soil. At each stage, he applied the knowledge of traditional wine-growing that he had acquired on his family's property, Vieux Château Certan.

The harvest, conducted entirely by hand, is again manually sorted before the grapes are crushed and destalked. Fermentation takes place at a high temperature to concentrate the flavor, while the maceration lasts for three weeks during which time the juice is pumped through several times. The maturation is "mixed,"

gradually re-established its reputation, and when Yves Armand took his father's place in 1985 he put all his energy into implementing the most advanced growing techniques and practicing the selection essential to the making of a great wine.

The wines of Château La Rame, the flagship of its AOC, have a delicate bouquet and a structure that combines strength and finesse. Creating a sensation of harmony and elegance, La Rame is a match for the greatest sweet white wines.

Rivers

Because of their great length and width, the rivers that crisscross the departement—the Garonne, the Dordogne, and the Gironde—create microclimates which affect or strengthen the prevailing Atlantic climate. Because of this, they play an all-important role in the region's viticulture.

Banks of the Gironde.

■ SAINT-ÉMILION & SAINT-ÉMILION GRAND CRU (A.O.C.)

Known as much for its architecture as for the excellence of its wines, Saint-Émilion dates from the Middle Ages. An interesting and unusual town, it has been listed as a world heritage site by UNESCO.

It is a jewel-box of old stone, built on a picturesque half-circle of hills facing the Dordogne valley. Its steep and narrow streets, its Roman and Gothic churches, its convents and cloisters all point to its prestigious past.

The main monuments still visible are the grotto of the hermit, Saint Émilion, which faces the remains of his disciples' monastery; the catacombs; and, next to these, the monolithic church, one of France's largest underground churches.

Not far from these marvels are the Tour du Roy, the collegiate church, the

Saint-Émilion cloister.

Cardinal's Palace, the Great Wall, the Cordeliers' convent, the ramparts, the moat, and the old wall which surrounds the city.

It was Edward I, King of England, who defined the jurisdiction of Saint-Émilion in letters of patent given at Condat in 1289. He divided it into nine parishes which today cover the following eight communes: Saint-Émilion, Saint-Étienne-de-Lisse, Saint-Christophe-des-Bardes, Saint-Sulpice-des-Faleyrens, Saint-Laurent-des-Combes, Saint-Pey-d'Armens, Saint-Hippolyte, and Vignonet. More than 800 *crus* within these eight communes are entitled to either the Saint-Émilion or the Saint-Émilion *Grand Cru* AOC. The production criteria for the second are much stricter than for the first. The terms *Grand Cru Classé* and *Premier Grand Cru Classé* are reserved for wines that have been officially classified (in this region, classification is subject to revision every ten years) and that meet the production requirements of the Saint-Émilion *Grand Cru* AOC. Louis XIV compared Saint-Émilion wines to the nectar of the gods. Despite the region's complex variety of soils, the wines fall into three or four categories, with classified growths in the first three.

— Those produced on the hillsides are rich and require aging; in this group are Châteaux Ausone, Bélair*, Beau Séjour Bécot, and La Couspaude.

— Those produced in the north-west part of the region, an area of gravel mixed with sand, are a little less rich, but their nose is lighter and finer, recalling that of the nearby region of Pomerol*. Among these are Cheval-Blanc* and Figeac.

— Those of the southern-exposed lower slopes and the clay-sand terraces are a little less rich and lighter, but with a developed nose. One of many in this group is Château Larmande.

— Those produced on the newer sandy terraces sloping down towards the plains of the Dordogne are silky, smooth, and perfumed, and can be appreciated in their youth. Most are entitled to the Saint-Émilion AOC, while a few particularly well-placed vineyards produce wine of high enough quality regularly to obtain the title Saint-Émilion *Grand Cru*.

SAINT-ESTÈPHE

Mill at
Saint-Estèphe.

■ Saint-Estèphe (A.O.C.)

The Saint-Estèphe commune is one of the most northerly of the Haut-Médoc*. It enjoys an exceptional location along the Gironde, which is visible from most of the hilltops that make up this region.

The commune's first known activity dates from the Middle Bronze Age, and its first vines were planted during the Roman occupation. As with other privileged wine-growing communes of the Médoc*, Bordeaux wine merchants have played a key role in establishing the region's reputation by storing and promoting the sale of its wines. The main estates were created in the eighteenth and nineteenth centuries. Today, small and medium-sized estates are again being grouped to create larger properties.

This hilly region's gravelly outcrops, consisting of quartz and stone mixed with light and sandy soil, have excellent natural drainage. This is reinforced in the south by the Saint-Vincent channel, which takes the water of the Lafite marsh to the estuary, and in the north by the Mappon canal, which carries the water of the Vertheuil marsh.

This commune has five *crus* classified in 1855, including Château Montrose* and Château Cos Labory, and many *Crus Bourgeois* such as Phélan Ségur, Ségur de Cabanac, Haut-Marbuzet*, and les Ormes de Pez.

Among Médoc* wines, those of the Saint-Estèphe appellation have one of the most distinctive characters: a robust body with a certain finesse, an ample tannic structure, and rich aromas of berries and spices. The size of this AOC

and the diversity of its soils and subsoils allow it to produce a remarkable variety of wines. Because of their robust nature, these wines need time before they can be fully appreciated.

■ Saint-Georges-Saint-Émilion (A.O.C.)

The old commune of Saint-Georges had a rich history before being joined to Montagne-Saint-Émilion in 1973. This exceptional site looks out over an impressive panorama. Many charming old houses, several old water mills, and a few monuments make the area worth visiting. In 1843, archeological digs uncovered magnificent Gallo-Roman remains near Château Saint-André. The church is of Roman primitive style; it contains naive sculptures,

and parts of it are Carolingien dating from the ninth century. In the Middle Ages, Saint-Georges was a barony with its own château, an overhanging fortified town under the jurisdiction of the Albret duchy. In 1773 the architect Louis transformed the château into magnificent Louis XVI style, which has been perfectly preserved.

Also worth looking out for are the *crus* of Château Calon, and Château Tour du Pas Saint-Georges.

The Saint-Georges-Saint-Émilion appellation is bordered on the south by the Barbanne stream, which separates it from Saint-Émilion*, and on all other sides by the Montagne-Saint-Émilion* AOC.

Saint-Georges-Saint-Émilion wines have a rich, deep, and dense purple color. They are fruity in their youth and become increasingly complex as they age; they have a well-developed structure, plenty of body, and are fat (well-fleshed) in the mouth. Their tannins* are very velvety.

■ Saint-Julien (A.O.C.)

The Saint-Julien parish has existed since the seventh century according to some historians,

Château Talbot, classified in 1855.

the eighth according to others. In its early days the parish was in the archdiocese of Moulis.

Known as Saint-Julien-de-Reignac, the commune changed its name to Saint-Julien-Beychevelle in the first half of the twentieth century, adding the name of the small port and hamlet whose activity contributed to the wine's fame. During the seventeenth century a few aristocrats and well-informed owners discovered the *terroir*'s exceptional wine-growing potential.

This commune, practically in the center of the Haut-Médoc*, is separated from Cussac in the south by marshland created by two streams originating in the Saint-Laurent region. Rising up from the Beychevelle* marsh is the attractive gravelly crest of Beychevelle, and on the northeast is the Saint-Julien* hilltop, separated from Pauillac* by the Juillac stream.

Saint-Julien is known above all for the remarkable consistency of its vineyard, located in the commune's center.

This forms a rectangle about 5 km long and 3.5 km wide, made up of Garonne gravel outcrops dating from the early Quaternary. At the western end, the soil has less gravel and more sand as the vineyard nears the forest.

Thanks to its topography and soil structure, Saint Julien's *terroir** is very well drained and perfectly suited to wine-growing.

It is not surprising, then, to find in this appellation five Second Growths classified in 1855, including Léoville Las-Cases and Ducru Beaucaillou*, and six other classified growths including Château Beychevelle* and Château Talbot. Between them, these eleven *crus* account between them for eighty percent of Saint-Julien's wine production! Châteaux Moulin de la Rose, de la Bridane, and Gloria are among the *Crus Bourgeois* that add to the AOC's fame.

Saint-Julien-Beychevelle was the first Bordeaux commune to enter its wines in a tasting*, first held in 1973, which could earn them a diploma. Saint-Julien AOC wines stand out for their beautiful color, their body, the richness of their fruit, and above all for their characteristic nose: suave and harmonious, with exquisite finesse. Some say that Saint-Julien wines represent the middle ground between the characters of Margaux* and Pauillac* wines: this is undoubtedly true and is mainly due to the nature of Saint-Julien's subsoil. Like all great Médoc wines, these wines are long lived, and age enhances their quality.

■ Sainte-Croix-du-Mont (A.O.C.)

A picturesque site and an exceptional *terroir** for the production of great sweet white wines. For the visitor this region is one of the most agreeable in Bordeaux. Its glorious vineyards produce incomparable wines, each with its own qualities.

An integrated collection of vineyards growing on hillsides that are often steep, makes up the Sainte-Croix-du-Mont wine-growing area. The nature of the soil and the grape varieties planted, along with the same harvest and vinification techniques used in Sauternes, allow the region to produce—weather permitting—first-rate sweet white wines.

Sainte-Croix-du-Mont wines have a sweetness, fruit, vigor, and elegance which could satisfy the most discerning and delicate palate. Their quality varies, of course, depending on the care that goes into the growing and, even more importantly, the harvest and vinification. As with all sweet wines, age amplifies their nose and flavor. Among the châteaux that hold the most promise for wine-lovers are La Rame*, Bel Air, and des Mailles.

White wines produced in the Sainte-Croix-du-Mont appellation area are currently entitled only to the Bordeaux Supérieur* or Bordeaux* AOC, even though this region is within the area defined by the Premières Côtes de Bordeaux*.

Sainte-Croix-du-Mont.

■ SAINTE-FOY-BORDEAUX (A.O.C.)

The ancient walled town of Sainte-Foy-La-Grande was founded in 1255 by Alphonse de Poitiers, a brother of Saint Louis, to protect its inhabitants from frequent invasions by the English. Though Sainte-Foy-La-Grande has never produced a drop of wine, it has given its name to this appellation. The town has played a role in the wine trade thanks to its location next to the Dordogne river, which has allowed the transport of many types of goods including wine from the hinterland.

As this appellation requires specific grape varieties and stricter production conditions than those of the Bordeaux* AOC, most of the region's growers prefer to use the Bordeaux appellation.

A few owners, though, are trying to revive the Sainte-Foy-Bordeaux appellation. Those who adhere to a charter created by the local wine-growers' union commit themselves to selecting the best land parcels, using growing methods that respect the vine and its environment, harvesting the grapes at their peak of ripeness and health, and respecting the winemaking standards of this AOC. Châteaux l'Enclos, de Vacques, and Hostens-Picant are noteworthy members of this group.

Rich or supple, with a complex nose of red berries, leaf mold, and leather, the red wines can be enjoyed young for their fruitiness and also improve with age. Their harmonious and tannic structure allows them to mature well in Bordeaux oak casks*. The dry and sweet white wines have floral and spicy aromas.

■ SAUTERNES (A.O.C.)

The region defined by the Sauternes AOC consists of five communes: Sauternes, Fargues, Bommes, Preignac, and Barsac*. This is the region that produces the precious nectar known throughout the world as Sauternes, considered by many enthusiasts to be the world's best white wine. The ultimate Sauternes wine is Château d'Yquem, which in 1855 was the only Gironde wine to be awarded the title *Premier Cru Supérieur*.

Like Cérons*, this wine-growing region is included in the southern part of Graves*.

It is separated from the Graves region on the west by the pleasant, green Ciron valley, which serves as a border for the Sauternes, Bommes, and Preignac communes. On the north, this valley separates Preignac from Barsac.

The type of soil and subsoil gives a particular character to the wine produced, which explains the slight differences between wines of different *crus*. Workers pick the grapes bunch by bunch, selecting the fruit that has been affected by the famous "noble rot", which is the key to Sauternes wines. This rot is caused by the fungus *Botrytis cinerea**.

Other than the judicious choice of grape varieties, it is the painstaking care that goes into the picking and winemaking, and above all this privileged region's nature and climate, that make Sauternes wine exceptional. Its marvellous color and clarity, sweetness and special, unique, incomparable depth make Sauternes more than a wine: it is a liqueur, an essence, a nectar that can be compared to

nothing but other Sauternes wines. Whatever their size or reputation, the vineyards are tended carefully so that during the harvest—no matter what surprises the weather might hold—grapes can be picked that are perfectly healthy and botrytized, which is essential for rich and concentrated must.

The Sauternes AOC currently has twenty-seven *crus* classified in 1855, ten of these in the Barsac commune: one *Premier Cru Supérieur*, Château d'Yquem, eleven *Premiers Crus* including Château Guiraud* and Château La Tour Blanche, and five *Seconds Crus*. Other *crus* produce high-quality wines, such as Châteaux de Fargues,

Raymond-Lafon, Haut-Bergeron, and Saint-Amand.

Despite their diversity—the result of their *terroirs** and growers—these wines are characterized by their deep gold color, their smoothness, roundness and calm power, and an unusual roasted quality. Their aromas bring to mind citrus, acacia, and apricot in a complex symphony.

Rich in glycerol and other sugars, they are very sweet, and often leave "pearls" on the side of the glass. In fact this is the ideal sweet white wine—as one poet put it, it is "extravagantly perfect."

These are wines that need to be put in the cellar and forgotten: over the years, they acquire a smoothness, body, and breeding that is uniquely their own. However, they can also be appreciated in their youth (after at least three years) for their liveliness, vigor, and fruit.

Great sweet wines can be enjoyed on their own, without food, as an apéritif or for sheer pleasure. Contrary to what many people believe, though, sweet wines and especially Sauternes can also accompany an entire meal.

These wines complement many foods: foie gras, delicate fish, butter and cream sauces, poultry and other white meats, blue and washed-rind cheeses, and desserts that are not too sweet.

Serving wine

At one time the glasses used for fine wines, especially Bordeaux, were small and were filled nearly to the brim. Today, fortunately, much larger sizes are used and the glass is filled only one-third full, which makes tasting much easier*.

To serve Bordeaux wines the preferred glass is the tulip, which has an oval shape. These generally have a large capacity of twenty-five to thirty centiliters. Glasses for drinking Sauternes* and other sweet white wines are a little smaller: eighteen to twenty centiliters.

Decanters should have a curved shape, without sharp angles, and above all should not be colored. The neck should be narrow (like a swan's neck) and have a glass stopper. Their capacity should be about one liter if they are to hold the contents of a normal bottle, and a little more than one-and-a-half liters for a magnum.

Seuil (Ch. du)

Dating from the eighteenth century, Château du Seuil is one of the most beautiful residences in Cérons*. An exceptional position on the banks of the

Garonne makes the property especially attractive. Well situated on the plateau of Larrouquey, the vines benefit from a gravelly or siliceous-clay-limestone soil on a rocky bed and produce excellent quality Graves* wines which regularly win awards in various competitions.

Château du Seuil.

Mr. and Mrs. Robert Watts and their daughter bought this estate in 1988 and have put a great deal of work into restoring and developing the vineyard, which currently covers twelve hectares (four of these produce white wine).

In their quest for quality, they have installed a number of temperature-controlled stainless-steel vats. These are complemented by a cellar that can hold 250 oak casks for maturing the wine. Dry and sweet white wines are matured in new casks.

Tannin

This is a group of organic substances found in the seeds, skin, and stems of grapes. It contributes to the aging potential of red wines, which have more tannin than white wines.

Grape must.

Corks: the key to storage.

Map of the city of Bordeaux in 1550: Father Patrice-John O'Reilly, nineteenth century.

▮ Tasting

Tasting is an art, a science, and a pleasure. It is also an inexhaustible subject of conversation, even disagreement. Whole books have been devoted to it, both theoretical and technical, but also peppered with amusing anecdotes.

Bordeaux wine-lovers taste these wines at every opportunity. Calling on all five senses, the taster holds the glass by the stem; touch comes into play, and the choice of glass becomes all-important. A blind tasting should be thought of as a game. It is better to tell guests which wine you're serving, as knowing what you're tasting is an integral part of the pleasure. Next come sight, smell, and taste, which help us appreciate the color, the nose, the fruit, and finally, the body of the wine.

■ TERROIR

One of the most complex wine terms, this is often reduced to its geological aspect. The word "*terroir*" refers not only to the soils and subsoils of a *cru** or an AOC, but also the climate, production methods, history, and customs that have led to the creation of the *cru* or appellation*.

■ TONNEAU

A traditional measuring unit of production of a Bordeaux estate. One *tonneau* is equivalent to four Bordeaux oak casks*: 900 liters, 1,200 bottles, or 100 cases.

■ Tour Haut-Caussan (Ch.)

Château Tour Haut-Caussan has an excellent seventeen-hectare vineyard, planted with fine grape varieties: half Cabernet and the other half split between Merlot and Malbec.
It produces an average of 100,000 bottles of Médoc* AOC wine, half of which is sold in France to a particularly faithful clientele and the other half exported.

Half of this vineyard grows on the slopes and crest of a hill near the village of Caussan. The soil, which is rocky at the top and gravelly on the lower slopes, is ideally suited to wine-growing. The other half grows on gravel in Potensac.
The current owner ensures that the viticulture and vinification are carried out with the utmost care. Philippe Courrian is especially attentive to the maturing process: the wines are matured in oak barrels (one-third new) for one to two years, depending on the character of the vintage.

Château
Tour Haut-Caussan
1995

CRU BOURGEOIS
MÉDOC
APPELLATION MÉDOC CONTROLÉE
750 ML
12,5 % vol
L 050
PHILIPPE COURRIAN
VITICULTEUR À BLAIGNAN, MÉDOC - GIRONDE
MIS EN BOUTEILLE AU CHATEAU

The Malagar property.

Tourism

Each year more than four million visitors come to the Gironde for its 125 kilometers of sandy beaches, 450,000 hectares of forest, nearly the same area of lakes, and 115,000 hectares of vineyards. Following in the footsteps of the French writers François Mauriac and Montesquieu, who explored wine-growing regions, tourists find a site or an estate to visit in each commune. The more they see, the more they come to realize that wine is not just a product but an integral part of the region's culture.

Union des Grands Crus

This association brings together about a hundred *crus** of the Médoc*, Graves*, Saint-Emilion*, Pomerol*, Sauternes*, and Barsac*. These *crus**, whether classified or not, have joined up to promote their wines. The Union Charter, of which an extract is quoted here, states the philosophy of its members:
"A *Grand Cru* of the Union is located on a particular *terroir**, limited and original, capable of

producing a highly personalized wine with exceptional aging potential. Attached to this *terroir* are storage tanks and cellars equipped for traditional methods of vinification and maturation, supervised by the proprietor of the estate.

A Union *Grand Cru* should have facilities for welcoming visitors in a way which reflects the tradition of hospitality associated with Bordeaux's wine-growing châteaux.

The name of the *cru* has been sanctioned by history and cannot be dissociated from its *terroir*: it is guaranteed by the name stamped on the cases, corks, capsules, and labels."

View of Bordeaux harbour in the nineteenth century.

1997

Vieux Château
GAUBERT

GRAVES
APPELLATION GRAVES CONTRÔLÉE
12,5% Vol.   S.C.E DOMINIQUE HAVERLAN, VITICULTEUR A PORTETS - GIRONDE   750 ml
L VC59 87.1   MIS EN BOUTEILLE AU CHATEAU

■ VIEUX CHÂTEAU GAUBERT

Originally from Portets, the Gaubert family made its fortune in the shipping industry during the eighteenth century. In 1796, the merchant Gaubert decided to enlarge his country house and create a large vineyard. He hired the architect Gabriel Durand, a colleague of Victor Louis, architect of the Grand Théâtre de Bordeaux. Durand kept the original eighteenth-century architecture, enlarged the house and in the park built a number of outbuildings for the production of wine from the estate.

Located in the center of Portets, this residence could easily have been demolished. Luckily for the commune and the Graves region, it was listed as a historic building and acquired by Dominique Haverlan, which allowed the building to be saved and the vineyard restored. A winegrower's son and himself a grower, Dominique Haverlan studied oenology in depth before creating his own vineyard within the family property in 1981. He bought, rented, grouped together and planted several parcels of land with a total surface area of about twenty hectares in Portets and Beautiran.

By 1983, his vineyard had outgrown the family property's facilities and he transferred the vinification to magnificent storehouses on an old wine-growing estate. He created a cellar for maturing the wines in oak casks, which increased their quality. In 1988, the acquisition of Vieux Château Gaubert and its restoration gave the property a more prestigious image which fits perfectly with the wines it produces. With their styles and qualities—the reds have an intense, full, and rich nose, while the whites are powerful, ample, velvety, and fruity—these wines are among the most representative of the Graves* AOC.

Typical *Graves* appellation soil.

▦ WINE TRADE

The term *négoce* is used to describe the commercial companies in the Gironde that market Bordeaux wine, in France and abroad, to an extremely diverse and ever-growing clientele. Historically, the wine trade of the Gironde has always played an important role in spreading the reputation of Bordeaux wines around the world. Its heyday goes back to the end of the eighteenth and beginning of the nineteenth century, when a large number of wine merchants, most of them Anglo-Saxon or Scandinavian, settled in the Chartrons district of Bordeaux, on the left bank of the Garonne.

Their cellars stretched along the river, which was the only means of transport for shipping wines abroad. The offices and private residences looking out over the river were soon to become one of the finest collections of urban architecture in eighteenth-century Europe.

The wine trade's main role is to contribute to the knowledge of the wine market—to keep track of consumers' tastes and expectations and to match these with the range of wines available in Bordeaux.

But it also plays a role in stabilizing the market. Wine is by definition a natural product, and certain factors such as quality, availability, and price are difficult to predict. Wine traders have traditionally taken pressure off the growers by buying their wines young and storing them in their modern cellars, which have a total bottling capacity of 4.5 million hectoliters and a storage capacity of three million hectoliters. Thanks to these facilities, a vast range of wines can easily be made available to buyers.

More than 300 businesses, 200 of them traditional wine merchants/growers who store wine on their premises, make up this formidable machine. Though the wine trade is less powerful than it once was, its turnover is about $2.3 billion, with exports accounting for thirty-seven percent of this figure.

Les Chartrons (nineteenth century) drawn by Philippe; lithograph by Armand Cuvillier.

■ Yquem (Ch. d')

This estate belonged to the de Sauvage family from the sixteenth century until 1785, when Alexandre de Lur-Saluces married the last de Sauvage heiress. Count Alexandre de Lur-Saluces took over as head of the property in 1968. Since the marriage of Louis-Amédée in 1785 to the "very great and powerful dame Joséphine," he is the sixth generation of Lur-Saluces to run this estate, which has been blessed by nature and made a shining example by its owners.

The Yquem domaine consists of 188 hectares, 113 hectares of which are under vine (each year about 106 of these produce wine in a rotating system). The exceptional quality of the wines is due to the particular nature of the soil—a drainage system was added as the subsoil is often clay—and to the hills' admirable exposure, the strict selection of grape varieties, and the obsessive care that goes into the cultivation, harvest, and vinification. This is one of the most rigidly controlled estates in the Sauternes: it is planted with eighty percent Sémillon and twenty percent Sauvignon (Muscadelle was voluntarily removed), and the vines are severely pruned. The leaves are carefully thinned out and the harvest is carried out with the most meticulous attention to detail—some think this is the key to Yquem's greatness. Great care also goes into the vinification: the must is always fermented in new oak casks and

remains there until the wine is racked and bottled, usually in February or March of the fourth year after the harvest. Only the part of the harvest which is judged to be perfect will be bottled with the name Château d'Yquem—in some years, such as 1964, 1972, 1974 and 1992, no wine was sold as Château d'Yquem.

It is this constant attention and devotion to the quality of the wine that allowed Yquem, in the 1855 classification, to be ranked first among the firsts, as it was the only wine to be awarded the title *Premier Cru Supérieur*. Today it is still the leader among the great wines of Sauternes* and the world's best white wine.

On average, each vine at Yquem produces a single glass of wine, for an average of 95,000 bottles a year. Some years, the property produces a small amount of dry white wine made with fifty percent Sauvignon and fifty percent Sémillon and calls it Ygrec, which recalls the name of its big brother Yquem.

Since April 1999, the LVMH group has held 64 percent of shares in Château d'Yquem.

Château d'Yquem, *Premier Cru Supérieur* classified in 1855.

CHÂTEAUX
When dialing from outside France, drop the initial zero after the country code (33).

Château Bélair
33330 Saint-Émilion
Tel.: 05 57 24 70 94

Château Belgrave
Groupe C.V.B.G.
35 rue de Bordeaux
33290 Parempuyre
Tel.: 05 56 35 53 00

Château Beychevelle
33250 Saint-Julien
Tel.: 05 56 73 20 70

Château Bonnet
33420 Grézillac
Tel.: 05 57 25 58 58

Château Closiot
Closiot
33720 Barsac
Tel.: 05 56 27 05 92

Château Côte Montpezat
B.P. 42
33350 Belvès-de-Castillon
Tel.: 05 57 56 05 55

Château Ducru-Beaucaillou
33250 Saint-Julien-Beychevelle
Tel.: 05 56 59 05 20

Château d'Escurac
33340 Civrac-en-Médoc
Tel.: 05 56 41 50 81

Château Grand Mouëys
S.C.A. Les Trois Collines
33550 Capian
Tel.: 05 57 97 04 44

Château Guiraud
33210 Sauternes
Tel.: 05 56 76 61 01

Château Haut-Brion
133 avenue Jean Jaurès
33600 Pessac
Tel.: 05 56 00 29 30

Château Haut-Marbuzet
33250 Saint-Estèphe
Tel.: 05 56 59 30 54

Château Latour
33250 Pauillac
Tel.: 05 56 73 19 80

Château Latour Martillac
33650 Martillac
Tel.: 05 57 97 71 11

Château Maison Blanche
33570 Montagne
Tel.: 05 57 74 62 18

Château Margaux
33460 Margaux
Tel.: 05 57 88 83 83

Château Mondésir Gazin
33390 Plassac
Tel.: 05 57 42 29 80

Château Montrose
33180 Saint-Estèphe
Tel.: 05 56 59 30 12

Château Moulin Haut-Laroque
33141 Saillans
Tel.: 05 57 84 32 07

Château Mouton Rothschild
33250 Pauillac
Tel.: 05 56 59 22 22

Château Nodoz
33710 Tauriac
Tel.: 05 57 68 41 03

Château Poujeaux
33480 Moulis-en-Médoc
Tel.: 05 56 58 02 96

Château Puygueraud
33570 Saint-Cibard
Tel.: 05 57 56 07 47

Château La Rame
33410 Sainte-Croix-du-Mont
Tel.: 05 56 62 01 50

Château du Seuil
33720 Cérons
Tel.: 05 56 27 11 56

Château Tour Haut-Caussan
33340 Blaignan
Tel.: 05 56 09 00 77

Vieux Château Gaubert
33640 Portets
Tel.: 05 56 67 52 76

Château d'Yquem
33210 Sauternes
Tel.: 05 57 98 07 07

WINE MERCHANTS

UNITED KINGDOM

John Armit Wines
5 Royalty Studios
105 Lancaster Road
London W11 1QF
Tel.: 020 7908 0600

Balls Brothers
313 Cambridge Heath Rd
London E2 9LQ
Tel.: 020 7739 6466

Bordeaux Index
3-5 Spafield St
London EC1R 4QB
Tel.: 020 7278 9495

Justerini & Brooks
20–21 Saint James Sq
London SW1Y 4JD
Tel.: 020 7484 6433

UNITED STATES

Ashbury Market
205 Frederick Street
San Francisco, CA 94117
Tel.: (415) 566-3134

Kermit Lynch
717 The Alameda
Berkeley, CA 94710
Tel.: (510) 524-1524

Morell & Company
1 Rockefeller Plaza

Scarsdale
New York, NY 10020
Tel.: (212) 688 9370

Sherry Lehman
679 Madison Ave
New York, NY 10021
Tel.: (212) 838 7500

Zacchy's
16 Parkway, Scarsdale
New York, NY 10583
Tel.: (914) 723 0241

INSTITUTIONS

**Académie des Vins
de Bordeaux**
1 cours du 30 Juillet
33000 Bordeaux
Tel.: 05 56 00 21 95

C.I.V.B
1 cours du 30 Juillet

33000 Bordeaux
Tel.: 05 56 00 22 66

**Fédération des Grands
Vins de Bordeaux**
1 cours du 30 Juillet
33000 Bordeaux
Tel.: 05 56 00 22 99

**Syndicat des négociants
en Vins et Spiritueux de
Bordeaux**
1 cours du 30 Juillet
33000 Bordeaux
Tel.: 05 56 00 22 90

**Union des Grands Crus
de Bordeaux**
10 cours du 30 Juillet
33000 Bordeaux
Tel.: 05 56 51 91 91

V I N T A G E S

This list classes the quality of Bordeaux wines since 1985.

Red wines

Excellent: 1985 - 1989 - 1990
Very good: 1986 - 1988 - 1995 - 1996 - 1998
Average: 1987 - 1994 - 1997
Acceptable to poor: 1991 - 1992 - 1993

Dry white wines

Excellent: 1985 - 1989 -1994 - 1995 - 1996 - 1998
Good: 1986 - 1987 - 1988 - 1990 -1993 - 1997
Meager: 1991 -1992

Sweet white wines

Excellent: 1988 - 1989 - 1990 -1995 - 1996
Very good: 1986 - 1997 -1998
Good: 1985 - 1991 - 1994
Meager: 1987 - 1992 - 1993

CLASSIFICATION OF GRAVES GROWTHS

COMMUNE	CLASSIFIED GROWTH	WINE TYPE	CURRENT OWNERS
Cadaujac	Château Bouscaut	red and white	Château Bouscaut Ltd.
Léognan	Château Carbonnieux	red and white	Société des Grandes Graves
Léognan	Domaine de Chevalier	red and white	Domaine de Chevalier Ltd.
Villenave-d'Ornon	Château Couhins	white	I.N.R.A. - Ministry of Agriculture
Villenave-d'Ornon	Château Couhins-Lurton	white	André Lurton
Léognan	Château Fieuzal	red	Château Fieuzal Ltd.
Léognan	Château Haut-Bailly	red	Robert G. Wilmers
Pessac	Château Haut-Brion	red	Domaine Clarence Dillon Ltd.
Talence	Château Laville Haut Brion	white	Domaine Clarence Dillon Ltd.
Léognan	Château Malartic-Lagravière	red and white	Château Malartic-Lagravière Ltd.
Talence	Château La Mission-Haut-Brion	red	Domaine Clarence Dillon Ltd.
Léognan	Château Olivier	red and white	Bethmann Ltd.
Pessac	Château Pape Clément	red	R.L. Montagne and Co. Ltd.
Martillac	Château Smith-Haut-Lafitte	red	Florence and Daniel Cathiard
Talence	Château La Tour-Haut-Brion	red	Domaine Clarence Dillon Ltd.
Martillac	Château La Tour Martillac	red and white	Kressmann GFA

CLASSIFICATION OF SAINT-ÉMILION GROWTHS
CLASSIFIED IN 1996

PREMIERS GRANDS CRUS CLASSÉS

CRUS	CURRENT OWNERS	COMMUNE	NATURE OF SOIL
Château Ausone	Vauthier family	Saint-Émilion	Hill and plateau
Château Cheval-Blanc	Mr. Arnaud and Mr. Frère	Saint-Émilion	Gravel and old sand
Château Angélus	Mr. Boüard and Mr. de Laforest	Saint-Émilion	Lower slope, old sand
Château Beau-Séjour (Bécot)	Beau-Séjour Ltd.	Saint-Émilion	Hill and plateau
Château Beauséjour	Duffau-Lagarosse heirs	Saint-Émilion	Hill
Château Bélair	Mrs. J. Dubois-Challon	Saint-Émilion	Hill and plateau
Château Canon	Ch. Canon Ltd.	Saint-Émilion	Hill and plateau
Château Figeac	Mr. and Mrs. T. Manon-court	Saint-Émilion	Gravel and old sand
Clos Fourtet	Lurton Brothers and Sister	Saint-Émilion	Plateau and old sand
Château La Gaffelière	Count de Malet-Roquefort	Saint-Émilion	Hill, lower slope
Château Magdelaine	Ets Jean-Pierre Moueix	Saint-Émilion	Plateau, hill and lower slope
Château Pavie	Mr. and Mrs. Perse	Saint-Émilion	Hill and plateau
Château Trottevieille	Castéja heirs	Saint-Émilion	Plateau

CRUS	CURRENT OWNERS	COMMUNE	NATURE OF SOIL
Ch. L'Arrosée	Château L'Arrosée GFA	Saint-Émilion	Hill
Ch. Balestard-La-Tonnelle	Capdemourlin GFA	Saint-Émilion	Plateau
Ch. Bellevue	Château Bellevue Ltd.	Saint-Émilion	Hill and plateau
Château Bergat	Castéja heirs	Saint-Émilion	Hill and plateau
Ch. Berliquet	Viscount and Viscountess Patrick de Lesquen	Saint-Émilion	Plateau and hill
Ch. Cadet-Bon	Château Cadet-Bon Ltd.	Saint-Émilion	Plateau and hill
Ch. Cadet-Piola	Jabiol GFA	Saint-Émilion	Plateau and hill
Ch. Canon-La Gaffelière	Counts von Neipperg	Saint-Émilion	Lower slope
Château Cap de Mourlin	Capdemourlin GFA	Saint-Émilion	Hill and old sand
Ch. Chauvin	Béatrice Ondet and Marie-France Fevrier	Saint-Émilion	Old sand
Ch. La Clotte	Chailleau heirs	Saint-Émilion	Hill
Ch. La Clusière	Mr. and Mrs. Perse	Saint-Émilion	Hill
Château Corbin	Domaines Giraud Ltd.	Saint-Émilion	Old sand
Château Corbin-Michotte	Mr. Jean-Noël Boidron	Saint-Émilion	Old sand
Château la Couspaude	La Couspaude GFA	Saint-Émilion	Plateau
Couvent des Jacobins	Joinaud-Borde	Saint-Émilion	Old sand
Ch. Curé-Bon	Château Curé-Bon GFA	Saint-Émilion	Plateau and hill
Ch. Dassault	Château Dassault Ltd.	Saint-Émilion	Old sand
Château La Dominique	Mr. Clément Fayat	Saint-Émilion	Old sand and gravel
Ch. Faurie-de-Souchard	Jabiol-Sciard GFA	Saint-Émilion	Lower slope

GRANDS CRUS CLASSÉS

CRUS	CURRENT OWNERS	COMMIUNE	NATURE OF SOIL
Ch. Fonplégade	Armand Moueix	Saint-Émilion	Hill
Ch. Fonroque	Ch. Fonroque GFA; J.A. et J.J. Moueix	Saint-Émilion	Hill and old sand
Château Franc-Mayne	Axa Millésimes	Saint-Émilion	Hill
Ch. les Grandes Murailles	Société des Grandes Murailles	Saint-Émilion	Hill and old sand
Ch. Grand-Mayne	Mr. Jean-Pierre Nony	Saint-Émilion	Hill and old sand
Ch. Grand-Pontet	Château Grand-Pontet Ltd.	Saint-Émilion	Hill and old sand
Ch. Guadet-Saint-Julien	Mr. Robert Lignac	Saint-Émilion	Plateau
Ch. Haut-Corbin	Haut-Corbin Ltd.	Saint-Émilion	Old sand
Château Haut Sarpe	Mr. J. Janoueix	St-Ch.-des-Bardes	Plateau and hill
Château Clos des Jacobins	Domaines Cordier	Saint-Émilion	Hill and old sand
Ch. Lamarzelle	Carrère Edmond GFA	Saint-Émilion	Old sand and gravel
Ch. Laniote	Arnaud and Florence de la Filolie	Saint-Émilion	Old sand
Ch. Larcis-Ducasse	Mrs. Hélène Gratiot-Alphandery	St-L.-des-Combes	Hill and lower slope
Ch. Larmande	La Mondiale	Saint-Émilion	Old sand
Ch. Laroque	St.-Christophe-des-Bardes GFA	St. Ch.-des-Bardes	Plateau
Château Laroze	Meslin Family	Saint-Émilion	Old sand
Château Matras	Château Matras GFA; V. Gaboriaud-Bernard	Saint-Émilion	Lower slope
Château Moulin du Cadet	Ch. Moulin du Cadet Ltd.	Saint-Émilion	Hill and old sand

CRUS	CURRENT OWNERS	COMMUNE	NATURE OF SOIL
Clos de L'Oratoire	Counts von Neipperg	Saint-Émilion	Lower slope
Château Pavie-Decesse	Ch. Pavie-Decesse Ltd.	Saint-Émilion	Plateau and hill
Château Pavie-Macquin	Corre-Macquin heirs	Saint-Émilion	Plateau and hill
Ch. Petit-Faurie-de-Soutard	Mrs. F. Capdemourlin	Saint-Émilion	Old sand and hill
Château Le Prieuré	Baronne Guichard Ltd.	Saint-Émilion	Plateau and hill
Château Ripeau	Mrs. Françoise de Wilde	Saint-Émilion	Old sand
Ch. St-Georges Côte-Pavie	Mr. Jacques Masson	Saint-Émilion	Hill and lower slope
Clos Saint-Martin	Grandes-Murailles Ltd.	Saint-Émilion	Hill and old sand
Château La Serre	M. B. d'Arfeuille	Saint-Émilion	Plateau
Château Soutard	Ligneris Family	Saint-Émilion	Plateau and hill
Château Tertre Daugay	Count de Malet-Roquefort	Saint-Émilion	Plateau and hill
Château La Tour Figeac	Ch. La Tour-Figeac Ltd.	Saint-Émilion	Old sand and gravel
Ch. La Tour-du-Pin-Figeac	Giraud-Belivier GFA	Saint-Émilion	Old sand and gravel
Ch. La Tour du Pin Figeac-Moueix	Vnes Jean-Michel Moueix Ltd.	Saint-Émilion	Old sand and gravel
Ch. Troplong-Mondot	Valette GFA	Saint-Émilion	Plateau
Château Villemaurine	Château Villemaurine GFA	Saint-Émilion	Plateau
Château Yon-Figeac	Château Yon-Figeac GFA	Saint-Émilion	Old sand

MEDOC GROWTHS
AND THEIR OWNERS

FIRST GROWTHS

COMMUNES	GROWTH CLASSIFIED IN 1855	NAMES OF OWNERS IN 1855	CURRENT NAME OF CLASSIFIED GROWTH	NAMES OF CURRENT OWNERS
Pauillac	Ch. Lafite (1)	Sir Samuel Scott	Ch. Lafite Rothschild	Barons de Rothschild
Pauillac	Ch. Latour (1) &	Mr. de Beaumont Mr. de Courtivron Mr. de Flers	Ch. Latour	Mr. François Pinault
Margaux	Ch. Margaux (1)	Mr. Aguado	Ch. Margaux	Ch. Margaux Ltd.
Pauillac	Ch. Mouton	Baron N. de Rothschild	Ch. Mouton-Rothschild	Baroness P. de Rothschild Ltd.
Pessac	Ch. Haut-Brion (2)	Mr. Eugène Larrieu	Ch. Haut-Brion	Clarence Dillon Ltd.

(1) Classified a First Growth in 1855. (2) Graves Cru, classified a First Growth in 1855.

SECOND GROWTHS
(In alphabetical order of current names.)

COMMUNES	GROWTH CLASSIFIED IN 1855	NAMES OF OWNERS IN 1855	CURRENT NAME OF CLASSIFIED GROWTH	NAMES OF CURRENT OWNERS
Cantenac	Ch. Brane	Baron de Branne	Ch. Brane-Cantenac	Mr. Lucien Lurton
St-Estèphe	Ch. Cos-Destournel	Mr. Martyns	Ch. Cos-d'Estournel	Jean Merlaut
Saint-Julien	Ch. Ducru-Beau-Caillou	Mr. Ducru-Ravez	Ch. Ducru-Beaucaillou	Borie Family
Margaux	Ch. Vivens-Durfort	Mr. de Puységur	Ch. Durfort Vivens	Mr. Gonzague Lurton
Saint-Julien	Ch. Gruau & Laroze	Mr. de Bethman Baron Sarget Mr. de Boisgérard	Ch. Gruaud-Larose	Château Gruau-Laroze Ltd.
Margaux	Ch. Lascombe	Miss Hue	Ch. Lascombes	Bass Group
Saint-Julien	Ch. Léoville	Marquis de Las Cazes Baron de Poyféré Mr. Barton	Ch. L. Las Cases Ch. L. Poyféré Ch. L. Barton	Ch. Léoville Las Cases Ltd, Dne de St-Julien GFA, Mr. Anthony Barton
St-Estèphe	Ch. Montrose	Mr. Dumoulin	Ch. Montrose	Mr. J.-Louis Charmolüe

114

SECOND GROWTHS

COMMUNES	GROWTH CLASSIFIED IN 1855	NAMES OF OWNERS IN 1855	CURRENT NAME OF CLASSIFIED GROWTH	NAMES OF CURRENT OWNERS
Pauillac	Ch. Pichon-Longueville	Baron de Pichon Longueville	Ch. Pichon-Longueville, Ch. Pichon-Longueville-Csse de Lalande	AXA Millésimes, Mrs. M. E. de Lencquesaing
Margaux	Ch. Rauzan Ségla Gassies	Csse de Castel Pers, Mr. Viguerie	Ch. Rausan-Ségla, Ch. Rauzan-Gassies	Ch. Rausan-Ségla, Mr. Jean-Michel Quié

THIRD GROWTHS

(In alphabetical order of current names.)

COMMUNES	GROWTH CLASSIFIED IN 1855	NAMES OF OWNERS IN 1855	CURRENT NAME OF CLASSIFIED GROWTH	NAMES OF CURRENT OWNERS
Cantenac	Ch. Boyd	Several owners	Ch. Boyd-Cantenac Ch. Cantenac-Brown	Ch. Boyd-Cantenac GFA, Axa Millésimes
St-Estèphe	Ch. Calon	Mr. S. Lestapis	Ch. Calon-Ségur	Calon-Ségur Ltd; Ph. Capbern-Gasqueton
Margaux	Ch. Desmirail	Mr. Sipière	Ch. Desmirail	Mr. Denis Lurton
Margaux	Ch. Dubignon	Mr. P. Dubignon Mr. M. Dubignon	(no longer exists)	
Margaux	Ch. Ferrière	Mrs. Vve J. Ferrière	Ch. Ferrière	Château Ferrière Ltd.
Labarde	Ch. Giscours	Mr. Pescatore	Ch. Giscours	Nicolas Tari GFA
Cantenac	Ch. d'Issan	Mr. Blanchy	Ch. d'Issan	Ch. d'Issan Ltd.
Cantenac	Ch. Kirwan	Mr. Deschriver	Ch. Kirwan	Schröder & Schÿler & Co.
Saint-Julien	Ch. Lagrange	Count Duchâtel	Ch. Lagrange	Ch. Lagrange Ltd.
Ludon	Ch. Lalagune	Mrs. Vve Jouffroy-Piston	Ch. La Lagune	Mr. J.-Michel Ducellier
Saint-Julien	Ch. Langoa	Mr. Barton	Ch. Langoa	Mr. Anthony Barton
Margaux	Ch. Saint-Exupéry	Mr. Fourcade	Ch. Malescot-St-Exupéry	Mr. Roger Zuger
Margaux	Ch. Becker	Mr. Sznajderski & Mr. Rolland	Ch. Marquis-d'Alesme-Becker	Mr. Jean-Claude Zuger
Cantenac	Ch. Palmer	M. E. Pereire	Ch. Palmer	Château Palmer Ltd.

FOURTH GROWTHS

(In alphabetical order of current names.)

COMMUNES	GROWTH CLASSIFIED IN 1855	NAMES OF OWNERS IN 1855	CURRENT NAME OF CLASSIFIED GROWTH	NAMES OF CURRENT OWNERS
Saint-Julien	Ch. de Beychevelle	Mr. F. Guestier	Ch. Beychevelle	Grands Millésimes de France
Saint-Julien	Ch. Du-Luc	Mr. Du Luc Aîné	Ch. Branaire-Ducru	Château Branaire Ducru Ltd.
Pauillac	Ch. Duhart	Mr. Castéja	Ch. Duhart-Milon Rothschild	Duhart-Milon Rothschild Ltd.
St-Estèphe	Ch. Rochet	Mrs. Vve Lafon de Camarsac	Ch. Lafon-Rochet	Château Lafon-Rochet GFA
Margaux	Ch. Marquis-de-Thermes	Mr. Sollberg	Ch. Marquis de Terme	Château Marquis de Terme Sénéclauze Ltd.
Cantenac	Ch. Poujet-Lassale	Mr. Izan	Ch. Pouget	Château Pouget GFA
	Ch. Poujet	Mr. de Chavaille		
Cantenac	Ch. Le Prieuré	Mrs. Vve Pagès	Ch. Prieuré-Lichine	Ballande Group
Saint-Julien	Ch. Saint-Pierre	Mr. Bontemps-Dubarry Mrs. Vve Roullet Mrs. Vve Galloupeau	Ch. Saint-Pierre	Mrs. Françoise Triaud
Saint-Julien	Ch. Talbot	Marquis d'Aux	Ch. Talbot	Mrs. Rustmann-Cordier & Mrs. Bignon-Cordier
St-Laurent	Ch. Carnet	Mr. de Luëtkens	Ch. La Tour Carnet	Château La Tour Carnet GFA

FIFTH GROWTHS
(In alphabetical order of current names.)

COMMUNES	GROWTH CLASSIFIED IN 1855	NAMES OF OWNERS IN 1855	CURRENT NAME OF CLASSIFIED GROWTH	NAMES OF CURRENT OWNERS
Pauillac	Ch. Batailley	Mr. F. Guestier	Ch. Batailley Ch. Haut-Batailley	Castéja heirs, Mrs. des Brest-Borie
St-Laurent	Ch. Coutenceau	Mr. Bruno-Devez	Ch. Belgrave	Château Belgrave GFA
St-Laurent	Ch. Camensac	Mr. Popp	Ch. de Camensac	Château de Camensac GFA
Macau	Ch. Cantemerle	Mrs. de Villeneuve-Durfort	Ch. Cantemerle	S.M.A.B.T.P. Group
Pauillac	Ch. Clerc-Milon	Mr. Clerc	Ch. Clerc Milon	Baronne Philippine de Rothschild GFA
St-Estèphe	Ch. Cos-Labory	Mr. Martyns	Ch. Cos-Labory	Dom. Audoy Ltd.
Pauillac	Ch. Croizet-Bages	Mr. P. Calvé	Ch. Croizet-Bages	Jean-Michel Quié
Labarde	Ch. Dauzac	Mr. Wiebrok	Ch. Dauzac	M.A.I.F.
Pauillac	Ch. Artigues-Arnaud	Mr. Duroy de Suduiraut	Ch. Grand-Puy-Ducasse	Grand-Puy-Ducasse Ltd.
Pauillac	Ch. Grand-Puy	Mr. F. Lacoste	Ch. Grand-Puy-Lacoste	Borie Family
Pauillac	Ch. Haut-Bages	Mr. Libéral	Ch. Haut-Bages-Libéral	Haut-Bages-Libéral Ltd.
Pauillac	Ch. Lynch	Mr. Jurine	Ch. Lynch-Bages	Cazes Families
Pauillac	Ch. Lynch-Moussas	Mr. Vasquez	Ch. Lynch-Moussas	Castéja heirs
Pauillac	Ch. Darmailhac	Mrs. d'Armailhac	Ch. Mouton-Baronne-Philippe	Baronne Philippine de Rothschild GFA
Pauillac	Ch. Pédescleaux	Mr. Pédescleaux	Ch. Pédesclaux	Château Pédesclaux GFA
Pauillac	Ch. Canet	Mr. de Pontet	Ch. Pontet-Canet	Château Pontet-Canet GFA
Arsac	Ch. Le Tertre	Mr. Henry	Ch. du Tertre	Château du Tertre Ltd.

SAUTERNES AND BARSAC GROWTHS
WHITE WINES CLASSIFIED IN 1855

SUPERIOR FIRST GROWTH
(Presented in the order of the April 18, 1855 classification.)

COMMUNE	GROWTH CLASSIFIED IN 1855	NAME OF OWNER IN 1855	CURRENT NAME OF CLASSIFIED GROWTH	NAME OF CURRENT OWNER
Sauternes	Ch. Yquem	Bertrand de Lur-Saluces	Ch. d'Yquem	Ch. d'Yquem Ltd.

FIRST GROWTHS
(Presented in the order of the April 18, 1855 classification.)

COMMUNES	GROWTH CLASSIFIED IN 1855	NAMES OF OWNERS IN 1855	CURRENT NAME OF CLASSIFIED GROWTH	NAMES OF CURRENT OWNERS
Bommes	Ch. Latour Blanche	Mr. Focke	Ch. La Tour Blanche	Ministry of Agriculture
Bommes	Ch. Peyraguey	Mr. Lafaurie (Elder)	Ch. Clos Haut-Peyraguey Ch. Lafaurie-Peyraguey	Clos Haut-Peyraguet GFA, Dnes Cordier
Bommes	Ch. Vigneau	De Reyne widow	Ch. de Rayne Vigneau	Ch. de Rayne Vigneau Ltd.
Preignac	Ch. Suduiraut	Guillot Brothers	Ch. Suduiraut	Axa Millésimes
Barsac	Ch. Coutet	Bertrand de Lur-Saluces	Ch. Coutet	Ch. Coutet Ltd.
Barsac	Ch. Climens	Mr. Lacoste	Ch. Climens	Mrs. Bérénice Lurton
Sauternes	Ch. Bayle	Mr. Dépons	Ch. Guiraud	Ch. Guiraud Ltd.
Sauternes	Ch. Rieusec	Mr. Mayé	Ch. Rieussec	Ch. Rieussec Co.
Bommes	Ch. Rabaud	Mr. Deyme	Ch. Rabaud-Promis Ch. Sigalas-Rabaud	Ch. Rabaud-Promis GFA, Ch. Sigalas-Rabaud GFA

SECOND GROWTHS

(Presented in the order of the April 18, 1855 classification.)

COMMUNES	GROWTH CLASSIFIED IN 1855	NAMES OF OWNERS IN 1855	CURRENT NAME OF CLASSIFIED GROWTH	NAMES OF CURRENT OWNERS
Barsac	Ch. Mirat	Mr. Meller	Ch. de Myrat	Pontac Family
Barsac	Ch. Doisy	Mr. Deane	Ch. Doisy-Daëne Ch. Doisy-Dubroca Ch. Doisy-Védrines	E.A.R.L. Vnes P. &D. Dubourdieu Louis Lurton Ch. Doisy-Védrines Ltd.
Bommes	Ch. Pexoto	Lacoste widow	*now part of Rabaud-Promis*	
Sauternes	Ch. d'Arche	Mr. J & Mr. C. Lafaurie	Ch. d'Arche	Ch. d'Arche Ltd.
Sauternes	Ch. Filhot	Bertrand de Lur-Saluces	Ch. Filhot	Ch. Filhot GFA
Barsac	Ch. Broustet Nérac	Mr. Capdeville	Ch. Broustet Ch. Nairac	Laulan Family, Mrs. Nicole Tari
Barsac	Ch. Caillou	Mr. Saraute	Ch. Caillou	Mrs. and Mr. Pierre
Barsac	Ch. Suau	Mr. Pédesclaux	Ch. Suau	Mr. Roger Biarnes
Preignac	Ch. de Malle	Henry de Lur-Saluces	Ch. de Malle	Countess de Bournazel
Preignac	Ch. Romer	Mr. de Lamyre Mory	Ch. Romer Ch. Romer du Hayot	Mr. Guy Farges Vnes du Hayot Ltd.
Sauternes	Ch. Lamothe	Baptiste widow	Ch. Lamothe Ch. Lamothe-Guignard	Mr. Guy Despujols Mr. P .& Mr. J. Guignard

SELECTED BIBLIOGRAPHY

Broadbent, Michael. *Wine Vintages*. London: Antique Collectors Club, 1997.

Coates, Clive. *Grands Vins: the Finest Chateaux of Bordeaux and their Wines*. Berkeley: Uni. of California Press, 1995.

Collombet, François. *The Flammarion Guide to World Wines*. Paris: Flammarion, 2000.

Desseauve, Thierry. *The Book of Wine*. Paris: Flammarion, 2001.

Doraz, Michel. *Bordeaux: A Legendary Wine*. New York: Abbeville, 1998.

Parker, Robert. *Bordeaux: A Comprehensive Guide to the Wines Produced from 1961 to 1997*. New York: Simon and Schuster, 1998.

Peppercorn, David. *Wines of Bordeaux*. New York: Mitchell Beazley, 2000.

Robinson, Jancis. *The Oxford Companion to Wine*. New York: Oxford University Press, 1999.

Turnbull, James. *Bordeaux: The Ninety Greatest Wines*. Paris: Hachette, 1999.

Walraven, Hans. *Grands Crus de Bordeaux: A Comprehensive Pocket Guide*. San Francisco: Wine Appreciation Guild, 1998.

Photographic credits: Flammarion archives: p. 18, 78; Bordeaux municipal archives: 7, 16, 74 top, 98–99, 100–101 bottom; Barton et Guestier: 9, 14–15; J. P. Bost: 39; Burdin S.A.: 82; CDT 33, B. P. Lamarque: 4–5, 19, 33, 34 top, 50, 86–87; CIVB: 28–29, Gilles d'Auzac: 36, F. Mousis: 96–97, P. Roy: 42, 80–81; Château Belgrave: 23; Ch. Beychevelle: 24–25; Ch. Bonnet: 29; Ch. Chasse Spleen: 73; Ch. Cheval-Blanc: 35; Ch. Cloziot: 37; Ch. Côte Monpezat: 38 bottom; Ch. Ducru Beaucaillou: 44 top; Ch. d'Escurac: 46; Ch. Grand-Mouëys: 51; Ch. Guiraud: 54; Ch. Haut Brion: 55, 76–77; Ch. Haut Brondo: 54; Ch. Haute-Faucherie: 70–71; Ch. Haut-Marbuzet: 56 top; Ch. de Jayle: 10–11; Ch. Landiras: 52; Ch. Laroque: 47; Ch. Latour: 59; Ch. Latour Martillac: 60–61; Ch. Maison-Blanche: 64 bottom; Ch. Margaux: 67; Ch. Mont-désir Gazin: 70; Ch. Montrose: 72; Ch. Nodoz: 74 bottom; Ch. Pétrus: 82; Ch. Pichon Longueville: 57; Ch. Poujeaux: 79 bottom, 102–103; Ch. Puygueraud: 84 top; Ch. La Rame: 84 bottom; Ch. Saint-Georges: 89 bottom; Ch. du Seuil: 97 bottom; Ch. Talbot: 90; Ch. Tour Haut-Cassaudan: 99; Ch. Tour de Ségur: 66; Ch. d'Yquem, R. Dieth: 105; P. Cronenberger: 12–13, 20–21, 26–27, 33, 96 bottom, 48–49, 53, 62–63, 68, Editions Féret: 22, 61, 75, 88–89, photo E. Roger: 40, 43, 85; J. d'Hugues: 100–101 top; Musée d'Aquitaine, J. M. Arnaud: 6; B. Sirot: 17, 30, 37, 30–31, 41, 44–45, 56 bottom, 58, 64 top, 65, 83, 91, 92–93, 94–95; P. de Rothschild: 43; C. Tauzinat: 31; Vieux Ch. Gaubert: 102

Translated and adapted from the French by Rosa Jackson
Copy-editing: Gillian Delaforce
Typesetting: Julie Houis, À Propos
Color separation: Pollina S.A., France

Originally published as *L'ABCdaire des vins de Bordeaux* © 2000 Flammarion
English-language edition © 2001 Flammarion

ISBN: 2-08010-629-5
N° d'édition: FA0629-01-VII
Dépôt légal: 10/2001
Printed and bound by Pollina S.A., France - n° L84363

Pages 4–5: The village of Saint-Aignan, Bordeaux